THE ASIATIC DANGER IN THE COLONIES

THE ASIATIC DANGER IN THE COLONIES

L. E. NEAME

Routledge
Taylor & Francis Group

First published in 1907 by George Routledge & Sons, Ltd.

This edition first published in 2018 by Routledge
2 Park Square, Milton Park, Abingdon, Oxon, OX14 4RN
and by Routledge
711 Third Avenue, New York, NY 10017

Routledge is an imprint of the Taylor & Francis Group, an informa business

Publisher's Note
The publisher has gone to great lengths to ensure the quality of this reprint but points out that some imperfections in the original copies may be apparent.

Disclaimer
The publisher has made every effort to trace copyright holders and welcomes correspondence from those they have been unable to contact.

A Library of Congress record exists under ISBN: 7032192

ISBN 13: 978-1-138-60130-7 (hbk)
ISBN 13: 978-1-138-60152-9 (pbk)
ISBN 13: 978-0-429-46259-7 (ebk)

The day will come, and perhaps is not far distant, when the European observer will look round to see the world girdled with a continuous zone of the black and yellow races, no longer too weak for aggression, or under tutelage, but independent, or practically so, in government, monopolizing the trade of their own regions and circumscribing the industry of the Europeans.—*Mr Charles Pearson in 'National Life and Character.'*

. . . It is difficult to conceive any question at the present moment more momentous than the struggle between East and West for the inheritance of these semi-vacant territories. Promises have been made without knowledge or perception of the consequence involved in their fulfilment.—*Sir Arthur Lawley, Lieut.-Governor of the Transvaal,* 1904.

THE ASIATIC DANGER IN THE COLONIES

By

L. E. NEAME

LONDON
GEORGE ROUTLEDGE & SONS, LIMITED
NEW YORK: E. P. DUTTON & CO
1907

To the
Old Folks at Home

PREFACE

In the following pages an attempt is made to present a fair and impartial summary of the Asiatic difficulty as it affects the Colonies, and to justify the strong feeling which exists in the great outer areas of the Empire against this class of immigration. The opinions expressed will probably fail to give full satisfaction to either side. In one quarter they may be considered somewhat weak and nerveless ; in another they may be regarded as arguments in favour of a policy of spoliation and injustice. Upon this question it is peculiarly difficult to appreciate one's opponent's case. That colour prejudice which is reflected in the fourth article of the old Boer Grondwet may prevent the Australasian and the Africander taking an absolutely fair view of the Asiatic or British-Indian case. But the recent speeches of Anglo-Indians who accompanied the deputations to Lord Elgin and Mr Morley argue a similar intellectual myopia. Unwittingly I may also be afflicted with one disease or the other. Still the views hereafter expressed are the product of six years spent in

Asia and South Africa, and no one can possess a greater admiration for India and the Indian peoples. A decision against Asiatic immigration in the Colonies is in no way due to a lack of appreciation of Asiatic virtues—it is rather a testimonal to Asiatic capacity for succeeding.

To those who make a special study of Colonial affairs, the information given may contain nothing new. But there are many people who watch keenly the tendencies of the Empire who have not the time to devote to the somewhat laborious pastime of reading blue books and official papers. To these I hope the points emphasized will be helpful in arriving at a clearer appreciation of the Colonial attitude. Many of the facts have appeared from time to time in the columns of the *Empire Review*, the *Daily Mail*, the *Pall Mall Gazette*, the *Pioneer* (Allahabad) the *Rand Daily Mail*, and other journals, but the information is now re-arranged and amplified. For any shortcomings I must plead the difficulty of obtaining, in this part of the world, several works of reference desired.

Whilst this little record was in the press there arose a widespread anti-Asiatic agitation which supports many of the contentions set out. The storm produced by the Transvaal Asiatic Law Amendment Ordinance; the opposition to Indian immigrants in British Columbia; the dispute between Japan and the United States concerning the school regulations in San Francisco; the drastic anti-Asiatic legislation introduced in the Natal House of Assembly; the decision of the Chinese Government to again inquire into the working of the Australian laws and the subsequent re-assertion of the guiding principles of Australian and New Zealand policy; the outcry in Jamaica against Chinese store-keepers and hotel-keepers—all these incidents drive home the very real importance of the question.

But this agitation strengthens rather than modifies the argument that in the best interests of the Empire, the Colonies must be kept free from Asiatic immigration. In this connexion the word Colonies is used in its stricter meaning, and is not intended to apply to those parts of the Empire which are better described as Plantations. But I include the tropical parts of Australia and South Africa for reasons which Professor J. W. Gregory stated in his paper on "The Economic Geography and Development of Australia" which appeared in the *Geographical Journal* in September, 1906. The peace of the white man in the tropics can hardly be regarded as finally settled, despite the Cayenne disaster and other failures. However, whatever the ultimate decision may be on this point, the broad principle remains that the enormous areas suitable for white colorization in Africa, Australia, and North America should be closed to the Asiatic nations, whether British subjects or not. When an English Prime Minister talks of "twelve millions on the verge of starvation" and Commission after Commission reports on emigration schemes, it is surely essential to reserve these lands for the expansion of our own nation and peoples who blend with it.

The much condemned Asiatic Law Amendment Ordinance in the Transvaal was conceived in this spirit. There was no desire to inflict additional hardship upon the British Indian population. The idea was simply to establish once and for all the rights of the Indians already in the Colony. "Registration," Lord Milner told the Transvaal Indians in May, 1903, "gives you a right to be here, and a right to come and go. Therefore to me registration seems a protection to you as well as a help to the Government, and in any law passed I should like to see registration included." But it must be admitted that the British-Indian contention that the existing safeguards were ample without re-registration carried a good deal of weight. The special report on the Permit System drawn up at Lord Milner's request at the close of 1903 proved that there was "no large number of unauthorized Asiatics in the

Colony"—indeed only *two* Asiatics are mentioned as being found without permits. Again Lord Milner told the Indians that "once on the register your position is established, and *no further registration is necessary, nor is a fresh permit required.*" Yet within three years re-registration, with the taking of finger impressions, is demanded. It is certain that the first Parliament in the Transvaal will attempt to pass new legislation against Asiatics, but it is doubtful if the Home Government will assent. The British Indians were taken over with the other burdens of the Colony, and probably little can be done save rigorously to exclude a further influx—unless the principle of buying them out be adopted.

The Japanese protest regarding the San Francisco schools raises another difficult point, and a similar controversy must sooner or later arise in a British Colony. At the moment Colonial feeling sides with the people of the Pacific Slope.

The agitation which South Africa's anti-British Indian legislation arouses in India, and the possibilities of friction with the Eastern Powers upon similar grievances in Australasia, are unfortunate, but there seems to be little prospect of a satisfactory compromise.

All one can suggest is that the whole question should be discussed at the Imperial Conference in

London in April next (when India will be represented) with the idea of seeing whether Colonial feeling favours the appointment of a Royal Commission, representative of the whole Empire, to frame a policy which would obviate the constant recurrence of the friction of the past few years. But it would have to be recognized from the outset that the Colonies would never agree to any lowering of the barriers now erected against Asiatic immigration. Why the Colonies feel compelled to adopt such an attitude I have tried to explain in the following pages.

L. E. N.

P. O. Box 3996,
JOHANNESBURG.

CONTENTS

CHAPTER I

AN EMPIRE PROBLEM

CHAPTER II

THE VALUE OF THE ASIATIC

CHAPTER VI

THE CASE OF AUSTRALASIA

CHAPTER VII

SOME OF THE DANGERS

CHAPTER I

AN EMPIRE PROBLEM

OF all the problems which face the British Colonies to-day, none presents more difficulties or excites stronger feeling than that of the status of the Asiatic. Unfortunately it is not a local question, capable of settlement by purely local legislation. The final word in the control of the native races lies with the Imperial Government: in the case of the Asiatic this reservation is even more important. The political changes of the last five years have raised the position of the Asiatic into an Empire problem—perhaps even a World problem. It is complicated by Great Britain's alliance with an Asiatic Power; it is affected by the fact that millions of the Eastern races are British subjects and claim the privileges which the Empire boasts it confers; it calls into question—by contrast—the morality of our past policy in the East, and emphasizes the divergence between promise and practice found in our own territories to-day.

In England the question is looked upon as something remote, a theory for academic discussion and the application of abstract principles, rather than a vital problem calling for a practical solution. Few people realize how closely it may affect the Mother Country. Lord Durham said that the great waste lands of the Empire were "the rightful patrimony of the English people, the ample appanage which God and nature had set aside in the New World for those whose lot had assigned them but insufficient portions in the Old."[1] But unrestricted Asiatic immigration must inevitably limit the capacity of the outer areas of the Empire to absorb her surplus population; it means a serious check to the growth of England's trade with a large section of the colonies; it might easily lead to a commercial war which would cripple half her manufactures.

Old ideas of Asia must be modified to-day. One is still inclined to judge the East by the Chinese wars and the futilities of Chinese administration. One is still apt to cherish the belief that a beneficent Providence has placed the white nations for ever in an economic position which can never be seriously assailed. But there are already apparent the beginnings of a renewal of the old struggle between West and East. Only it is assuming a new form. The real Asiatic Peril is the acquisition, by commercial pressure and trade treaties, of the right of entry to lands now closed. It will be a repetition, less brutal, and probably slower and more subtle, of the policy of Europe towards Asia in the nineteenth century. The cloud to-day is no bigger than a man's hand. In a generation it may darken the whole political horizon.

The Englishman who has never lived in Asia, or

[1] "Report on Canada."

in a country in which there has been a considerable influx of Asiatics, does not grasp two things. It is not easy to convince him that the Asiatic inevitably underlives and undersells the white man. It is not less difficult to make him understand that Asiatic immigration cannot be classed with any other. It differs essentially from the lowest class of European immigration. The alien problem in England is simplicity itself contrasted with the Asiatic question in Africa or Australasia. The masses of Southern and South-Eastern Europeans who have entered the United States will in time be absorbed in the population. The process may take a varying length of time with different nationalities; but in the end there emerges the American people, even if their national character becomes modified by the infusion of alien blood. But no white race can absorb the Asiatic. The Eastern peoples always remain apart. You can never get rid of what Meredith Townsend called "the dull, unconquerable, unmitigable distaste of Asiatics for white men." It is not unreciprocated. Deep down beneath the strongest ideas of theoretical justice and the desire to admit no prejudice, there is a similar barrier. At the moment when Europe rang with the praise of Japanese valour, capacity, and high qualities, a baron, a naval captain, and a University professor—cultured men trained to Western ways—complained publicly of the "humiliating circumstance" they were subjected to on a steamer of one of the great European lines.[1]

[1] Baron Suyematsu's letter to the *Times*, January, 1906.

The social chasm between the natives of India and the white men who rule widens instead of closes. The line which is so rarely crossed is more marked to-day than it was a century ago. Ignoring for a moment the effect of Asiatic immigration upon the white man's work, it is well to realize that the introduction of a considerable number of Eastern people means that the difficulties of administration increase. Particularly is this the case in a country which already possesses a large native population. Natal finds the problem of the Bantu sufficiently complex without having to face a body of Asiatics more numerous than the white men, who remain, and always will remain, distinct.

But before considering the question in detail, there is another factor which must be included in a broad survey of modern conditions. We have the competition—what this really implies will be shown later. We have this separation, this racial barrier, which means that the Asiatic population must always remain apart. But in addition we have the awakening of Asia, a movement which involves a keener resentment than obtained in the old days of that which is regarded as unjust. There is a vague yet growing sense of commercial power. The idea is gaining ground that a weak spot has been found in the armour of Europe. The Swadeshi movement in India, foolish and inadequate as was its excuse, quasi-political as was its motive power, and rapid as was its decline, was not without significance. Still more important was the boycott of American goods in China; for the very energy with which the United States protested proclaimed a moral victory for the East. A lesson was learned which will not be forgotten. To-day it is seen how and where a blow can be struck. A lever has been found which may be used for the forcing of many a closed door. Asia, be it remembered, is in the strong position of the purchaser. Self-contained, self-supporting without hardship to her people, she can, if need be, dispense with the manufactures of Europe and America. But to the Western nations, ever increasing their manufactures, ever demanding more raw material and more markets for that which they make, the supplying of the myriads of the East is a matter of vast importance. "External markets," said Mr. Balfour recently, "are now more than ever necessary."[1] And, after all, "it is better to sell at ten per cent. to Hindoos or Chinese than at forty per cent. to the people of Brazil." To-day India buys more from England than any other part of the Empire: the aggregate purchases of Asia from the white nations are anywhere between one hundred and two hundred millions sterling a year. Yet this trade is only in its infancy. The simple wants of the Asiatic are slowly increasing. He relies more and more upon the supplies of Europe, allowing many an indigenous industry to languish. Competition for this trade grows yearly keener. Here lies the danger to the Colonies—the temptation to

[1] February 13, 1906.

the Home Government. What if a quarrel threaten with some Asiatic purchaser because a closed door is found in some not too well known colony ? What if a concession is likely to reward the nation which gives way a point in admitting the Asiatic to some distant land. Could those at Home who are crying out for markets resist the temptation of gaining an advantage even at the sacrifice of the interests of a colony thousands of miles away, and in defiance of the wishes of a people whose ideals are not understood ? These are points which must not be overlooked. In the agitation against Chinese immigration in Australia in 1888, Lord Knutsford, the Colonial Secretary, remarked in a telegram to Sir W. C. F. Robinson (South Australia): "Having regard to political and commercial interests of Empire, and particularly to commercial interests of Australasian Colonies, no avoidable obstacles should be placed in the way of trade with China, which is likely to afford valuable market for products of Australasian Colonies."

The danger is not an imaginary one—it is increased by ignorance of the real effect of Asiatic competition on a white race. For Asia, too, needs room for her surplus population. The checks of war have gone, the ravages of pestilence and famine grow yearly less ; but the races multiply as freely as ever. The population of Southern India is doubling itself in 88½ years. The cultivated area grows at the rate of 7·94 per cent. in a decade. But there is a limit to the land available. Subdivision cannot go on indefinitely. There must be an outward movement. How long can the barriers erected by the Western nations withstand the pressure—the pressure of political exigencies, the pressure of commercial ambition, the pressure of the demand of the thinly peopled lands for cheap labour? There is a growing irritation amongst British Indians at the restrictions now imposed. One of the best informed writers [1] who urge the claims of the Indian community in South Africa recently said:—

> "Are three-quarters of the population of the Empire to be aggrieved by reason of British breach of faith? Are the 'frontiers of the Empire' to be endangered by the dissatisfaction of three hundred millions of his Majesty's Indian subjects because Imperial pledges are disregarded and Imperial promises are callously broken at the bidding of a few fanatical provincials? Is India to become a menace to the Empire because its people are debarred from their rightful share in the privileges and responsibilities of British citizenship in any part of the King's dominions? How long will the East bear such treatment?"

The claims of the British Indians in the colonies are urged with a good deal of energy by the Indian National Congress Party both in India and England. Their arguments appeal peculiarly to Members of

[1] Mr. H. S. L. Polak, English Editor of *Indian Opinion*, in the *Empire Review*, June, 1906.

Parliament who know India but not the Colonies; they are the joy of those who always rush to the support of any one who opposes the Colonies, whether they are Zulu rebels or undesirable aliens. The suggestion that Englishmen who happen to live in a Colony are capable of managing their own affairs is denounced as pandering to the vices and brutalities of a degenerate race. There has of late been a growth of the spirit of interference —despite the laying down of some excellent principles by Lord Elgin—and if this policy continues a conflict with the ever increasing strength of Colonial Nationalism is inevitable. The extraordinary campaign of calumny against the Colonists in Natal bodes ill for a satisfactory solution of the Asiatic question.

The problem, from a Colonial standpoint, is this :—

Can we safely admit the Asiatic ?

What is the effect of this immigration ?

Are restrictive measures essential, and if so, where ?

These are the questions which must be faced. They are problems of peculiar importance to the British Empire, and they are problems upon which some definite policy is essential.

One great Colonial land lies within the sphere of influence of the most enterprising and the most overcrowded of the Eastern Powers ; another is already largely dependent on Asiatic labour, and yet complains that the white man is being displaced by the

British Indian and the Chinaman. These lands are suitable for white men ; intended, one might almost say, to relieve the pressure on England. Are they to become the homes of powerful white nations, adding to the strength of the British Empire, refuges for those who find that the Mother Country has no adequate place for them ; or are they to be lands in which a diminishing white population is condemned to a hopeless struggle for bare existence against an ever growing mass of Asiatics—people loyal to the Empire, thrifty, law-abiding, hard-working, if you like, but people who can never do the work for great Britain which would be done by white men ? Years ago Professor Seeley wrote : "Now that Great Britain is already full, it becomes fuller with increased speed ; it gains a million every three years. Probably emigration ought to proceed at a far greater rate than it does, and assuredly the greatest evils would arise if it were checked." The danger of checking this outward movement, at least to the British Colonies, exists to-day.

The first essential to a calm discussion of the Asiatic difficulty is to eliminate the question of colour. Admitting that a self-governing Colony has the right to say who shall cross its borders, it has no moral right to impose petty restrictions on an educated man because his skin happens to be brown. One must get away from the Colonial attitude of classing the Asiatic with the rawest of "red blanket" Kaffirs. That there can never be union —hardly sympathy—between the white and the coloured races I admit. But the cause is not colour, though colour may be in most cases the outward sign. The British Indian is often as light complexioned as the Southern European ; the Chinaman is sometimes whiter than the Colonial. Yet the instinctive dislike to union remains—that almost undefinable something which always has existed and always will exist. But the old distinction of colour will have to be abandoned if the question is not to give rise to ever increasing friction. One must face the fact that in the future the Eastern nations will negotiate with the West on different lines to the diplomacy of half a century ago. The new methods cannot be conducted on the basis of the resolutions of the National Convention of Asiatics at Pretoria. Lord Milner clearly saw the danger when he said to the first congress of municipal bodies in the Transvaal in 1903 :—

> ". . . The greatest danger of every sound policy is its exaggeration and its travesty, and if we are strongly and successfully to resist the influx of Asiatics into this country in a form in which it may endanger our civilization without appreciably relieving the over-population of other countries, I say again let us take the strong unassailable grounds of the social and economic reasons which exist for opposing that immigration, and do not let us base our opposition purely on the weak ground of colour. It is a matter of the very widest importance. The time may come when this Colony and South Africa generally may wish

to enter into relations, commercial or otherwise, with the rulers of the great Asiatic states —with British rulers in India, for instance, or with the native rulers of the great Empire of Japan. It is possible—it would be possible—for a South African statesman dealing with them to defend legislation restricting the indiscriminate influx into this country of Asiatics whom we do not want, of Asiatics of the low class, of Asiatics who come here to take the bread out of the mouth of white men who adequately perform the work that they would perform; but it would be impossible to enter into any sort of relation with the Asiatic world if we are going, in this country, to adopt sweeping and indiscriminate legislation against Asiatics, or, in upholding that legislation, to use language which is insulting to Asiatics as Asiatics."

The policy of Sir Harry Parkes, too, was based on the right principle when he said :—

> "They (the Chinese) are a superior set of people. We know the beautiful result of many of their handicrafts: we know how wonderful are their powers of imagination, their endurance and their patient labour. It is for these qualities I do not want them to come here. The influx of a few million of Chinese here would entirely change the character of this young Australian Commonwealth. It is because I believe the Chinese to be a powerful race,

capable of taking a great hold upon the country, and because I wish to preserve the type of my own nation in these fair countries, that I am, and always have been, opposed to the influx of Chinese."

This is the standpoint from which one must view the problem of the Asiatic in the Colonies—an economic standpoint. Looked at in this light, what is the history of this immigration, and what lesson does it teach ? Has the Asiatic been of value ? If so, do the advantages conferred by his labour outweigh the disadvantages of his competition ?

CHAPTER II

THE VALUE OF THE ASIATIC

"The greatest difficulty confronting the colonist from the earliest days of the Spanish West Indian settlements till the times of the Johannesburg gold mines of to-day has always been the scarcity and inconstancy of the labour supply."—EGERTON'S *Origin and Growth of the British Colonies.*

THERE is a tendency, especially in South Africa and Australasia, to refuse to admit that the Asiatic immigrant is of the slightest value. The matter is generally dismissed with a hasty declaration that an influx of Indians or Chinese is a "curse to the country." But a little investigation shows that this is not the case. Where this immigration is found to the largest extent the aliens did not creep in uninvited and unobserved. Their services were secured after careful consideration, and in many parts to-day the only regret is that greater numbers cannot be obtained. The shortage of unskilled labour is not some unusual product of twentieth century conditions, though probably the spread of education and civilization in their present forms will render the difficulty even more acute than it is to-day. The Commission sent out from Spain to inquire into the labour problem in the West

Indies dates back to 1517; in South Africa, where the trouble is now most marked, it began on that pleasant Sunday morning in April, 1652, when the *Dromedaris*, the *Goede Hoop*, and the *Reiger* cast anchor in Table Bay and Jan van Riebeek began to trade copper bars and tobacco with the Goringhaiquas and the Goraichouquas. It was van Riebeek who first propounded a scheme for importing Chinese into South Africa; it was Wagenaar, his successor, who in urging a similar proposal upon the Council of Seventeen, roundly declared that twenty-five industrious Chinese families would be of as much service to the Company as fifty families of such Europeans as were established at the Cape.[1]

To-day large tracts of the British Empire depend almost entirely upon the British Indian or the Chinese for their prosperity. The Chinese form the industrial backbone of the Straits, Malaya, and Borneo; Punjabis built the Uganda Railway; the Kanakas laid the foundation of the sugar industry in Northern Queensland; Chinese did much of the "spadework" on the western side of North America.

As an example of what Asiatic labour can do under the best conditions, take the case of the West Indies. Sixty odd years ago—after the liberation of the slaves—there was reached a crisis such as

[1] As late as 1874 and 1876 the Cape House of Assembly passed resolutions suggesting the importation of Chinese or Indian labourers.

that which forced the Transvaal to secure Chinese coolies for the Rand mines. Indeed the words of the House of Commons Commission of that time with regard to the West Indies might have been used to describe the condition of the Transvaal in 1903: "The principal causes of diminished production and consequent distress are the great difficulty . . . in obtaining steady and continuous labour, and the high rate of remuneration which they give for the broken and indifferent work which they are able to procure." The West Indies were saved by the British Indian. The conditions of contract were liberal, inducements were offered to the newcomers to settle in the country; and the West India Committee recently wrote of these immigrants:—

> "These coolies have become a most important and useful portion of the population. The Colony has derived incalculable benefit from their industrious and law-abiding citizenship, and they in turn have become prosperous to an extent hardly possible in their own country."

Professor Alleyne Ireland in his *Tropical Colonization* gives carefully prepared statistics proving that the West Indian Colonies which imported Asiatics have prospered far more than those which decided to rely upon their own inadequate and unreliable labour resources. Indian labour saved British Guiana and Trinidad from the economic stagnation of Dominica.

The history of Natal reveals a similar story. Nearly fifty years ago, when Sir George Grey, the

Governor of the Cape of Good Hope, visited Natal, the Durban Corporation presented an address which included the following passage :—

> " Independently of measures for developing the labour of our own natives, we believe your Excellency will find occasion to sanction the introduction of a limited number of coolie or other labourers from the East in aid of the new enterprises on the coast lands, to the success of which sufficient and reliable labour is absolutely essential ; for the fact cannot be too strongly borne in mind that on the success or failure of these rising enterprises *depends the advancement of the Colony or its certain and rapid decline.* Experimental cultivation has abundantly demonstrated that the issue depends solely on a constant supply of labour." [1]

The sanction asked for was granted. " Certain and rapid decline " was averted. The first shipment of coolie labour reached Natal on November 16, 1860. Much has happened since then in the history of the British Indians in the Garden Colony of South Africa. At one time the people of Durban went down to the harbour (as did the inhabitants of Sydney and Capetown in the days of the convict ships) prepared to resist the landing of the Indians by force. But to-day there is no cessation of the demand for indentured labour. Indian coolies work

[1] *Durban : Fifty Years of Municipal History.*—W. P. M. Henderson.

the sugar and tea estates of the coast; Indians develop the coal mines; Indians perform an increasing share of the work on the farms; for the farmers who at first viewed them with distrust are now as anxious to retain them as the planters. Since the advent of coolie labour the white population has more than doubled, the value of land has increased, the cost of living has gone down. It is the Indian coolie who gives Natal the cheap fruit and vegetables which are the envy of the Transvaal, who has brought under high cultivation large tracts which, but for his presence, would to-day be barren. The Umbilo Valley near Durban (recently swept by flood), and some of the land near Maritzburg, bear testimony to his industry. Mr. Maurice S. Evans, M.L.C., of Durban, who is now heading a movement for the cessation of indentured coolie labour, admitted in a little book he wrote some time ago, that the Indian is a better cultivator than the Kaffir, that he is steady, thrifty, and law-abiding.

In the case of the Transvaal the demand was equally strong. It is not my intention to review the labour problem in South Africa, or to attempt at this date to explain a situation which is so woefully misunderstood in England. But certain figures must be given to show the genuineness of the mine owner's claim that it was essential to indent upon Asia for unskilled labour. The Transvaal Labour Commission placed the labour shortage on the mines at 129,000, and estimated that an additional 196,000 labourers would be required in five years. Their figures for the Colony of the Transvaal alone were these :—

	Natives at work.	Natives still wanted.
Agriculture . . .	27,715	52,285
Mining	68,280	129,364
Other Industries .	69,684	No data available
Railways. . . .	16,250	39,750

This gave the shortage for the Transvaal alone at 221,399. Yet the Labour Commissioners found themselves forced to declare (the majority, at least, did) that "the belief which was so generally and confidently entertained that there is in Central and Southern Africa an ample supply of Native labour for all our needs, and that only organization and capital are necessary to secure it, has been completely dispelled." The South African Native Affairs Commission placed the shortage of unskilled labour in all British South Africa at 307,528. More than one-third of the gold industry of the Rand is now dependent on Chinese labour, and practically the remaining two-thirds on imported labour from Portuguese East Africa. To get rid of the indentured Chinese would mean the dismissal of 6,405 Europeans, the stopping of 3,135 stamps, and consequently the throwing out of operation of plant and machinery worth over eleven millions sterling.

The Chinese have saved the greatest industry in South Africa ; the British Indian has enabled Natal to prosper. And the demand is always greater than the supply. Natal agents "search every nook and corner" of Madras for immigrants willing to come to the plantations, and are forced to accept men who "do not compare favourably with the class of Indian recruited in years past."[1] British Guiana finds that its recruiting agents in Calcutta cannot obtain enough coolies to satisfy the requisitions of the planters—only 1,295 were indentured in 1904–5 against 2,932 in 1903–4—and talks of appointing an official in Madras also.

The value of cheap Asiatic labour is undeniable. By its aid colonies which seemed to be on the verge of ruin have prospered; new industries have been built up; invariably has it led to a more highly developed cultivation, to cheaper production, and to increased comfort for the white population. Yet this is not the last word. M. Leroy Beaulieu condemned the system as creating a new alien population with a different religion and different ideals of social life. Professor Egerton takes a similar stand. Writing of the West Indies, he says: "It was not until the introduction on a large scale of Asiatic coolies that the labour problem was, in a great measure, solved." But he added this reflection: "In a few generations it may be found that the importation of coolie labourers has in effect become a great measure of State-aided colonization."

And to show what that means in the great Colonies involves an inquiry into the effect of Asiatic competition in a country fitted for white men.

[1] Report of the Protector of Immigrants, Natal, 1904.

CHAPTER III

TERMS OF CONTRACT

We have seen that the presence of large numbers of Asiatics in certain Colonies has not been due to the Indians or Chinese pushing their way into lands where they were not desired. They have been recruited, actively searched for, at great trouble and expense, because their services were absolutely needed.

We have seen, too, that these services have been of immense benefit to the Colonies concerned. But it is necessary before considering the effect of this immigration on the white population, and its possible danger to the best interests of the Empire, to see under what conditions these Asiatics are obtained. This is really the crux of the whole question. Roughly there are two systems, the old indentures used in the West Indies, and the new contracts under which the Chinese have been brought to the Transvaal.

The chief differences are these :—

Transvaal.	West Indies.
1. The Chinese coolie in the Transvaal must not be employed in skilled labour.	1. The British Indian in the West Indies can be employed as a tradesman and

mechanic, or in other skilled work in the factory, during his indenture. There is no restriction whatever after his indenture ceases. During his indenture he frequently saves money and purchases cattle, which are looked after for him during his work at the estate.

2. The Chinese coolie in the Transvaal must be sent back to China at the termination of his indenture.

2. The British Indian in the West Indies has the option of remaining in the colony as a free man. He can receive Crown lands instead of his half return passage. He is encouraged to remain on the estate, where he receives free housing, medical attendance and pasture for his cattle.

3. The Chinese immigrant in South Africa may be accompanied by his wife or not at option.

3. The Indians in the West Indies must be accompanied by 40 per cent. of women.

The Natal indentures are, with a few exceptions, relating to the encouragement of coolies to remain in the colony, the same as those in the West Indies. In Natal the coolie who has completed five years on the estates or mines has three courses open to him :—

1. He can return to India.
2. He can re-indenture at a higher wage.
3. He can remain in the colony as a free man on paying a licence of £3 a year.

The case of contract labour in the Malay States need not be considered. The conditions are extremely varied, and the short sea passage makes work in the Straits peculiarly attractive to the Chinese. The wages are lower than in the Transvaal, but there are the additional inducements of being able to engage in trade on the termination of a period of service, and the possibility of acquiring property and land. A system of co-operation, in which the labourer shares in the profits of the venture, is also widely adopted, and very often the coolie has to buy his stores from the shop of his employer.

The effect of these different indentures is plainly visible in the population of the colonies concerned. In the West Indies and Natal the Government of India's conditions have resulted in a large permanent East Indian population. The immigrants are mainly lower class Madrassis and Bengalis, who find that they are much more comfortably off in their new homes than amidst the competition of overcrowded India. In the West Indies the land hunger of the Asiatic is easily satisfied, and if the man is enterprising enough, he can—as in Natal—become a trader. The result is that the indentured coolie stays as a free man. In Natal it is found that the number who return after the expiration of the first contract is only ten per cent., and the number going back at the end of a second term is still smaller. Natal to-day has 100,000 Indians; but 70,000 are free. British Guiana to-day has 105,000 British Indians in a population of 278,000; but only 20,000 are indentured on the estates. Jamaica has 12,500

British Indians; but only 1,819 are now indentured. Trinidad has 90,000 East Indians. In Fiji the Indians number 25,000. Between 1901 and 1904 they increased 5,685; but the native population *decreased* by 4,334. A *Times* correspondent wrote in 1906: "In the Fiji Islands it seems as if they (the Indians) are about to replace the natives and become the permanent population."

In accepting the Asiatic on the conditions of the West Indies and Natal, a colony resigns itself to an ever growing Asiatic population.

The difference between the forms of contract is vital. It destroys at once the arguments which are so often based upon a belief that the conditions in the West Indies and on the Rand are analogous. The white population of the Transvaal would never for a moment think of accepting Asiatic labour upon Trinidad conditions. The Transvaal system makes the indentures terminate in the land from which the coolies are drawn; it insists that they shall be engaged upon nothing save unskilled mine labour. Under the Rand contracts there is no competition with white men, no permanent trace would be left if the 50,000 odd coolies were repatriated to-morrow. The Chinese could work the Rand mines for a decade and then return to China, and not one white storekeeper or one white artisan would have been affected. Whatever the objections to Chinese indentured labour on the Rand may be, it is certainly not a system of "State-aided colonization," as is that under which Asiatics are obtained for Natal and the West Indies.

CHAPTER IV

ASIATIC COMPETITION

WHAT is the effect of a considerable immigration of Asiatics into another country ? This phase of the question is apt to be overlooked in England, where, as Sir Arthur Lawley pointed out some years ago, the climate forms a barrier to such an influx, and the amount of unskilled labour available is an additional safeguard. England cannot understand the anxiety with which South Africa and Australasia view the competition of the coloured races. It has had no experience of it.

The Asiatic invariably obtains a grip of the country he enters. He may arrive as the humblest hewer of wood and drawer of water, but he does not remain in this servile position—or at least his children do not. Mr. Maurice S. Evans, in his *Problems of Production in Natal*, says : " It is interesting to note that signs are present that the rising generation of Indians, born in Natal, differ from their parents, the indentured coolies. With some education they, not content with the plain work and hard fare of their parents, aspire to a higher social position, and are usually waiters, clerks, and storemen." This is the reason why the demand for Asiatic labour never ceases. Ten thousand may suffice to-day. But the leakage is great. At the end of the term of contract a great number turn to other vocations. The land hunger of the Indian impels him to obtain ground for cultivation ; or the spirit of the trader drives him to invest in a hawker's basket and continue his thrifty, hard-working life till he can establish himself as a petty storekeeper or even a merchant on a considerable scale.

Here again much depends on the great climatic difference which creates the two classes into which Asiatic labour falls—that of the tropical and the non-tropical colonies. In the tropics the white population with whom the British Indian or the Chinaman could compete is exceedingly small. There is no outcry against him, because the capacity of the tropics to provide employment for white men depends mainly upon the size of the coloured population. In the West Indies the Asiatic is encouraged in every possible way to become a unit of the country. In the year 1904 alone the British Indians in Trinidad purchased 4,898 acres of land.

But take the case of lands which are climatically suitable for supporting white populations, and study the result of Asiatic immigration, and one begins to understand why the feeling against the newcomers, even when their economic value as unskilled labourers is recognized, is so strong.

Natal forms the best example. Although the coast belt may be regarded as tropical, and therefore, perhaps, better for Asiatics as labourers than white men, the great bulk of the colony is eminently suited for white settlers. Mr. Maurice S. Evans writes: "As on the coast, all the manual labour on the up-country farms is done by natives or Indians, but not for any climatic reason or on account of any physical conditions. The up-country climate of Natal is a magnificent one for Europeans; the adult can enjoy perfect health, and families of children are reared as healthy and strong as country children of Northern Europe. Manual labour on the farm could well be done by Europeans, to the benefit and not detriment of their health and condition. The reason why this is not done is social and racial, and would probably rule if Natal, with her present proportion of blacks to whites, was situated 50 degrees north latitude instead of 30 degrees south. The white man will not work alongside or on even terms with the native or Indian; we must accept this fact as one unlikely to be altered, and in speaking of the present state of the country take it as an axiom. Formerly all these farmers employed natives exclusively, now many supplement the native by Indians, or use the latter altogether."

The 1904 census in Natal showed that there was a total population of 1,108,754 classified as follows :—

	Males.	Females.	Total.
Europeans or whites.	56,758	40,351	97,109
Indians and Asiatics.	63,497	37,421	100,918
Mixed and others .	3,610	3,076	6,686
Natives in service .	69,746	10,232	79,978
Natives in native areas	357,020	467,043	824,063

The male Asiatics outnumber the male Europeans by 9,000 odd. And with what rapidity an Asiatic population grows when it is brought in under the conditions obtaining in Natal is shown by the following table :—

	Europeans.	Indians.
Census 1891	46,788	41,142
Census 1904	94,226	100,749

European increase . . . . 101·38 per cent.
Asiatic " . . . . 144·88 " "

Thus for every 100 Europeans in Natal in 1891 there are now 201·38, and for every 100 Indians there are now 244·88. The Census Committee comment: "It is appalling to consider what the Indian figures may be in the near future at this abnormal rate of increase as compared with the European races with our present Indian population of over 100,000."

There is however no slackening of the demand. In 1902 requisitions for 19,000 men were received, and in 1904 no fewer than 10,144 still remained to be allotted. At the end of 1905 applications for another 30,000 were received by the Indian Immigration Trust Board. The Protector of Indian Immigrants in his Report for 1904 states that the introductions of Indians into Natal in that year "far exceeded the number introduced for several years past." The birth-rate amongst the Indians is 30·71, and thus it is clear that if the importation of coolies proceeds at the rate reached in the past, the Indian population in Natal in 1916 will be over 250,000. The Indians who arrive in Natal prefer to remain there. The Protector reports: "The percentage of those who re-indentured during 1904, after completing their second term of indenture (being the first who have done so), is barely seven per cent., evidently indicating that the longer absence from India has had the effect of weaning the Indians from any desire to retain the privilege entitling them to a free passage back." The Indians who indenture only do so because a high wage enables them to save money to purchase land or to start as a trader. They do not re-indenture on the tea and sugar estates, where wages range from 16*s.* to 30*s.*, but prefer the coal mines, where they can earn from 40*s.* to 45*s.*

The hard-working Indian can prosper in Natal as he never could in Madras or Bengal. The bulk of the immigrants are of poor class, yet the 1,672 who returned to India in 1904 declared their savings at £20,077—and only 874 were men. Fifty-five had saved £100 or over. The average was £16 7*s.* 6*d.* as against £18 10*s.* 1*d.* in 1903, but the decrease was accounted for by the larger proportion returning as unfit for work. The average for indentured Indians alone exceeded that of 1903. In the Transvaal Legislative Council in 1903 Mr. Loveday estimated that £500,000 was sent out of the sub-continent every year by Asiatics to their relatives in the East.

But the bulk of the Indians do not return. Here is the Natal classification in 1904 :—

	Men.	Women.	Children.	Total.
Free Indians . .	20,318	10,077	26,581	56,976
Indentured . .	20,225	8,302	2,576	31,004
	40,543	18,280	29,157	87,980

It will be seen that the total given here is far below the total found in the Census report. The 13,000 odd additional must be classed with free Indians, for the number indentured is well known. This number "unaccounted for" is a more prominent feature of the Protector of Immigrants' Report each year.

What is the work done by this large body of ex-indentured labour ? Take first the case of agriculture. The Indian has a keen desire to purchase land, and when he obtains it he makes more use of it than either the white man or the Kaffir. That the price of fruit and vegetables at Durban and Maritzburg has gone down is due almost entirely to the cultivation of the Asiatics. But he is doing more than performing work which was formerly left undone. He is taking up work which, in the climate of Natal, could be and should be performed by the white man. The most important interest in Natal is the agricultural industry. In it, according to the last census, there are engaged 39,782 persons, divided as follows :—

Indians	32,436
Europeans	7,346

This is an extraordinary proportion. The tendency is brought out in other returns. For instance, 75·85 per cent. of the Asiatics are in the rural districts, whilst only 39·23 per cent. of the Europeans are so returned. Small wonder that even the cautious Census Committee, in reviewing the position indicated by these figures, remarks that this is "a condition of things regarded by many as distinctly opposed to the best interests of the Colony." The tables[1] dealing with occupations show how the grip of the Asiatic has affected agriculture. The most striking figures are appended :—

	Europeans.	Asiatics.
Cultivators	39	3,031
Farmers and assistants	6,606	2,412
Farm labourers	107	16,142
Fruit farmers	39	700
Gardeners	113	3,644
Fruiterers	17	151
Produce dealers	111	34
Poultry farmers	26	22
Planters (general)	96	133
Dairy farmers and assistants	131	20

It must be remembered that the heading Farmers and Assistants includes the 3,200 farmers who, according to the Government publication, *Notes on Agriculture in Natal*, hold a great deal of the land of the colony.

[1] This table and all others relating to Natal are compiled from the 1904 Census report, which was issued this year.

It is the Indian who supplies the bulk of the fruit and vegetables to the towns. Mr. Maurice S. Evans, whom I have already quoted—he is a public man who knows Natal from end to end, and has also travelled all over the world studying agricultural methods—says :—

> " . . . The Indian is a very much better cultivator of the soil than the native. Accustomed at home to small holdings and intensive culture, he brings his habits to Natal, and though in the presence of different conditions, of more space, less crowding, better markets, he varies his methods and perhaps gets more careless, he still obtains a larger share from his holdings in proportion to their size than the native or even the European. The Indian cultivators live principally on the coast, though they are now scattered all over the country in small numbers, wherever fertile land can be obtained not too far from a market. On the coast they grow principally mealies, beans, tobacco, bananas, some other fruits which come quickly into bearing, such as granadillas, and near the towns vegetables of all kinds. The Indian wants full value from his plot, and has no eye to scenic beauty, so he ruthlessly cuts down every tree or shrub upon it. He wants quick returns, hence as a rule does not plant fruit trees. From the nature of the crops grown and the absence of shade of all kinds, these lands have a bare sun-stricken appearance, detract from

the beauty of the country, and may possibly, if extended much more, have a deteriorating effect upon the climate.

" Indians both rent land and hold it freehold, and their holdings of both classes are extending year by year. Large areas in the coast country of Victoria, north of Durban, have of late years been acquired by syndicates of Europeans and retailed acre by acre to these people, who are keen to buy, and are willing to pay prices which no European could afford for occupation and cultivation. As a matter of fact, in this Garden County of the Garden Colony, the European population cultivating or in intimate connection with the soil is probably smaller in number than it was thirty years ago, while the Indian is gradually taking up the land upon which was reared in those days families of Europeans—colonists of the best stamp. What will be the outcome is causing anxious thought to many in Natal, who look beyond the present day and its present profit."

But the Asiatic has another fault—from the white man's standpoint. He is ambitious. The plantation coolie may die a coolie; his son may become a landowner, or a small trader or storekeeper, even a merchant on a considerable scale. In Natal Indian competition is not confined to agriculture. The loudest complaints come from the trading class. Practically the entire native trade in Natal has passed into the hands of the British-

Indians. The following figures show the position in respect to a number of trades in Natal in 1904 :—

	Europeans.	Asiatics.
Storekeepers (general)	658	1,260
Storekeepers' assistants . . .	1,252	1,323
Bakers and confectioners . . .	213	78
Butchers and assistants . . .	306	42
Grocers and assistants . . .	425	75
Restaurant-keepers	64	26

Even in clerical work the Asiatic has begun to make his presence felt. This is a department in which the figures will grow steadily as the Indians become more educated and the Indian children now at school begin to search for a means of livelihood.

To-day only 12,128 males of the 100,000 odd Indians in Natal can read and write. But they provide the following competition :—

	Europeans.	Asiatics.
Agents (various)	339	15
Accountants and bookkeepers . .	851	69
Clerks (various)	1,611	174
Civil servants	1,465	21
Commercial travellers	196	2

And lastly comes the general labour, skilled and unskilled, of the colony. One more table will show the trades or vocations in which the Asiatic is competing most keenly with the white man :—

	Europeans.	Asiatics.
Bricklayers and assistants . . .	1,056	122
Blacksmiths and assistants . .	523	30
Barmen	251	37
Brick and tilemakers	98	23
Boot and shoemakers	108	66
Barbers and assistants . . .	118	131
Brewers and assistants . . .	68	27
Bookbinders and assistants . .	47	13
Billiard markers	33	11
Carpenters and assistants . . .	2,328	196
Cooks	147	457
Coachmen and grooms . . .	92	117
Cycle dealers and mechanics . .	37	12
Carriers and carters	137	262
Cigar and cigarette makers . .	11	104
Domestic servants	1,083	2,132
Engine drivers (loco and stationary)	516	57
Fishermen	100	108
Firemen and stokers	652	257
Hawkers	19	1,487
Jewellers and assistants . . .	105	381
Labourers (general)	353	13,799
Labourers (railway)	164	610
Municipal employés	141	543
Messengers	3	99
Miners	208	185
Mineral water manufacturers and assistants	69	21
Mine labourers	—	600
Painters	661	79
Printers and compositors . . .	448	61
Plumbers and tinsmiths . . .	356	81
Photographers and assistants .	99	12
Porters (hotel and general) . .	96	133
Pumpmen (Natal railways) . .	1	32
Pointsmen (ditto)	—	138
Quarrymen	16	56
Tailors and assistants	266	126
Tobacconists and assistants . .	47	22
Waiters	100	658

It has been contended on behalf of the British-Indian population that the extent to which the progress of the white traders is hampered by this competition has been exaggerated. It would not be wise, perhaps, to adhere too closely to the census figures. In some cases they are open to explanations which tend to modify a first impression of the effect of Indian competition. But they show a marked tendency. They argue a not inconsiderable curtailment of the openings available for the white population. The British-Indians to-day own over 10,000 acres of land, and cultivate nearly 50,000 acres. As traders they would be a still greater menace, but for the Act passed in 1897 placing the power to issue or refuse general dealers' licences in the hands of an official of the Municipality. This measure was carried on the suggestion of Mr. Harry Escombe. Outwardly it carefully avoids class legislation, for in theory it applies equally to Europeans and Asiatics. But in practice it operates against the Indian storekeepers. No white man is refused a licence; Asiatics often suffer what they regard as injustice. There is no appeal from the decision of the Licensing Officer, and they can only protest and submit. In Durban the Act has been admittedly utilized in order to prevent Indian merchants opening shops in the principal streets. The Licensing Officer is the servant of a body of white storekeepers. He knows their views, and, whatever his personal opinion may be, he can hardly be expected to sacrifice his appointment by opposing those who employ him. As a protective measure to the white trader the Act is valuable. From the standpoint of expediency the system may find supporters. In reality it is simply class legislation. However, the point to be remembered is this. The state of things revealed by the Census would be even more marked but for an Act which was passed before the Indian community realized what its effect would be. How it operates may be seen from the following cases, reported in one of the leading European papers of the colony [1] :—

> "1. Mr. Hoondamal, who has been trading in the Colony for some time, wished to change premises, and to remove from Grey Street to West Street (Durban). The shop was absolutely free from objection from a sanitary standpoint. It belonged to an Indian landlord, and it was in a block of buildings which have been devoted to Indian traders for several years. Mr. Hoondamal had a fancy-ware business, and dealt in Oriental silks and other fancy goods. He did not come into competition with any European. His shop was kept in a scrupulously clean condition, but the transfer from one premises to another was rejected by the Town Council.
>
> "2. Mr. Dada Osman had been in trade in Vryheid for several years before the war. The place he was trading in was considered a location or a bazaar during the Boer *régime*. After Vryheid was annexed to Natal, the Licensing

[1] *Natal Witness*.

Board refused to renew his licence, unless he would go to another location far away from town, where it was impossible for him to do any business at all. Mr. Dada Osman's business in Vryheid has therefore proved a very serious loss to him. In this case, as also in the previous case, many certificates from Europeans of good standing were produced to show the respectability of the applicants. It should be remembered that Mr. Dada Osman's was the only Indian store in Vryheid. To add to the misery of the position, the anti-Asiatic laws of the Transvaal have been taken over bodily for this district of Natal. A British Indian, therefore, staying in Vryheid, not only has to undergo the disabilities that the Natal laws impose on him, but has added to them the disabilities that the Transvaal laws have created for him.

"3. Mr. Cassim Mahomed has been trading for three years on a farm near Ladysmith. For some time his was the only store. Recently, a European firm, by name Burdett & Co., have opened a store near by. Mr. Cassim Mahomed's servant, in his absence, was trapped and charged with a breach of the law as to Sunday trading, the servant having sold to the traps a piece of soap and a little sugar. Armed with this conviction, Messrs. Burdett & Co. opposed Mr. Cassim Mahomed's application for a renewal of his licence. The licensing officer listened to their objections, and refused to renew the licence. There was an appeal to the Board, which confirmed the decision of the Licensing Officer. The Court said that it was not guided by any prejudice: it proposed to treat Mr. Cassim Mahomed as it had treated a certain European. This was incorrect. This European was himself convicted of having sold opium, in contravention of the law, to the Indians working at the mines in his neighbourhood, and other allegations were made against him. There is an ocean of difference between the technical breach of the Sunday Law by the servant of Mr. Cassim Mahomed and the breach of the opium law of the Colony by the European personally. Mr. Cassim Mahomed, too, produced excellent references from European firms of good standing."

The paper also points out that when this Dealers' Licences Act was passed, the late Sir Henry Binns strongly protested against it, saying that it was an un-British measure, and that the ousting of the ordinary jurisdiction of the Supreme Court was a dangerous principle. "Experience has shown the justness of these prophetic words. The administration of the Act was, in its initial stages, marked by an excess of zeal in restricting British-Indian trade. The licensing officer at Newcastle refused to renew all Indian licences—that is, nine in number. It was after very great expense and trouble that six of them were renewed. As a result, and owing to pressure from the Colonial Office, the Government issued a warning to the licensing authorities that, unless they administered the Act with prudence and moderation, and respected existing licences, the Government might be obliged to amend the law, and restore the jurisdiction of the Supreme Court."

The law is undoubtedly harsh. But in attempting to estimate the extent of Asiatic competition it is necessary to point out that had no such legislation been passed the Indian storekeepers would be doing more of the trade of the colony than is the case to-day.

Eleven districts of the thirty-eight magisterial divisions or centres into which Natal is divided return no Indians. But in the Inanda Division the Indians form 70·58 of the population, in the Verulam Local Board area 52·83 per cent., in the Umlazi Division 34·44 per cent., and in the Lower Tugela 26·90 per cent.

Sir Arthur Lawley, when Lieutenant-Governor of the Transvaal, remarked in an official despatch: "So prevalent is the Indian element in that country (Natal) that the moment one crosses the Transvaal border he loses the impression that he is travelling in a European country at all. . . . Natal has an immense native population, which twenty years ago was served in the way of trade only by Europeans. Traders of this class formed an important element in the white population of Natal. To-day this class of trader has vanished altogether, and their business is now entirely in the hands of the Asiatics." It is claimed on behalf of the Indian community that this competition is trifling, that the Indian firm is but a "petty trader's concern." "The Indian storekeeper," said Mr. H. S. L. Polak, "acts as a connecting link between the native and the poor white on the one hand, and the wholesaler on the other; and as such is an invaluable economic factor in the commercial welfare of South Africa."

It is difficult to estimate what the extent of this "Kaffir truck" is. From a statistical standpoint the official publications relating to the natives all over South Africa are lamentably incomplete. A few sentences from the annual reports of the Resident Magistrates [1] throw some light on the point:—

Ixopo Division.—"During the last seven years several Asiatic retail licences have been cancelled and many applications refused."

Klip River Division.—"The bulk of the trade of the native population is still in the hands of the Indians, who appear to be gradually displacing the European traders."

Umgeni Divison.—"The bulk of the trade continues to be centred in the hands of the Indians and Indian hawkers. It is the Indians they principally deal with and dispose their surplus produce to."

Umvoti Division.—"In the country districts there are nine stores owned by Europeans and eleven by Asiatics."

Ndwedwe Division.—"I believe I am correct in stating that we are in the unique position of being the only Division in the Colony where the Asiatic has not gained a footing as a trader or retail dealer."

[1] Natal Blue Book on Native Affairs, 1904.

Newcastle Division.—" Most of the Kaffir storekeeping is in the hands of Indians and Arabs, who appear to have done a good business."

Inanda Division.—" The native trade of the Division is almost exclusively in the hands of the Indian and Arab storekeepers, who are not only in the villages but scattered all over the country ; and as natives are buying more and more European commodities, their requirements are ever on the increase, and the native trade must be a growing one."

Anything which induces the natives to display more energy and enterprise must be welcome, and few colonials object to the experiments which natives have made in storekeeping. In practically every case, however, the stores have failed, and in most instances the reason assigned in the Blue Book is that the native trader cannot compete with the Indian. It would appear, then, that the Asiatic immigrant is not only driving out the white trader, but is also checking a tendency on the part of the native which would hasten the spread of civilization. But in any case the Kaffir trade is not the small affair some people imagine. In 1903 the value of the goods imported into the colony of Natal for the Kaffirs was estimated at £302,778. The Kaffir is always charged heavily for his goods by the storekeeper, and a declared value of £300,000 for Customs purposes probably means that the goods were actually sold for £500,000 to £600,000. The Natal Industries Commission looked forward to a native trade based on an expenditure of £1 per head. This would mean roughly £1,000,000 from the Natal natives alone. Add to this the Indian coolie trade, and also that done with the poorer whites, and it is clear that the Indian traders are capturing a splendid field—and would have secured even more of it but for the restrictions mentioned, against which protests are raised. Zululand, too, is a closed land to the Asiatic trader, no licences being granted to non-Europeans. In considering the plea of the British-Indians that the volume of trade passing through their hands is trifling, one must do more than regard the trade done to-day—one must also allow for the increase which would be found in that trade if the restrictions (just or unjust) were swept away.

The figures relating to Asiatic competition in the other British Colonies in South Africa are less striking, because immigration has been restricted, and there has been no back door of indentured labour as has been open in Natal. Those who minimize this competition usually write as though these restrictions did not exist. Mr. Polak [1] estimates the proportion of *free* Indians in the whole of British South Africa as only one in sixty-two, and points out that there are eleven white people to every one Indian. This calculation is more ingenious than fair. It is obvious that excellent statistics, from the British-Indian standpoint, can be arrived at by taking the colonies in which Asiatic immigration is practically prohibited. But what would be the figures had there been no restrictive

[1] *Empire Review*, June, 1906.

legislation ? In Natal, simply through the contract system, by which an Indian can earn the right to remain by working five years for a European, the Indians already outnumber the whites. What would be the proportion in twenty years were the doors flung open, as some English publicists have suggested, and as apparently the Indian National Congress desires ? Even under the present system there will be 250,000 Indians in Natal in 1916. With the policy of the Open Door in all the colonies the proportion of eleven to one in favour of the European would one day be reversed.

To obtain the fullest information regarding Asiatic competition in the Cape Colony and the Transvaal one must await the issue of more complete returns than are now published. Certain statistics, however, are available which show the tendency is similar to that in Natal. In the Cape I leave out the Malay population of some 16,000, which is the result of the old slave trade.

The Asiatic traders in the Cape Colony manage, as in other parts, to exist through periods of depression which ruin many of the European storekeepers. The crisis through which the colony is passing is undoubtedly largely due to over-trading. The influx of traders has been greater than the growth of trade warranted, as will be seen by the following figures :—

INCREASE OF TRADERS.

	General Dealers.	Importers.	Agents.	Total.	Increase per cent. as compared with 1898.
1898	7,858	616	240	8,714	—
1902	11,137	1,036	346	12,519	43·7
1903	12,852	1,115	406	14,373	65·0
1904	13,444	1,032	319	14,795	69·7
1905	13,496	837	316	14,649	68·1

INCREASE OF TRADE.

	Importations retained in Cape Colony for consumption.	Increased per cent. over 1898.	Increase per cent. in number of licences granted over 1898.
1898	£10,481,000	—	—
1904	£12,832,000	22·4	69·7
1905	£13,096,000	25·0	68·1

The increase in the number of traders has been three times as great as the increase in the amount of trade. To throw the whole blame on the Asiatic would be absurd. The European was as much at fault. The point is that in these conditions the Asiatic holds his place whilst the European goes under.

In the five largest towns in the Cape Colony—Capetown, East London, King William's Town, Kimberley, and Port Elizabeth—the number of general dealers' licences issued to Europeans in 1905 was 5,222. But on May 1, 1906, only 3,920 Europeans had taken out licences. That is to say, 1,302 Europeans had been forced out of business. Now in 1905 there were 1,012 general dealers' licences issued to non-Europeans. But on May 6, 1906, there had been no decrease. On the contrary, the licences numbered 1,059. In these five towns, therefore, in one year, the increased competition had had the following effect :—

1. Licences to Europeans *decreased* 1,302.
2. Licences to non-Europeans *increased* 44.

In two years the Indian traders in the Cape sent to India £250,000 in money orders alone. And "despite the large number of Russian and Polish Jews in the country who are in the habit of remitting home very considerable amounts, the annual remittance to India through the Post Office exceeds that to the rest of the world put together, the United Kingdom included, without making allowance for the large proportion remitted to the Homeland in connection with the parcel trade." [1]

The European complains that it is impossible for him to compete with the Asiatic without lowering his standard of living—without, in fact, descending in the scale of civilization. Here is a sketch of the Indian trader's progress as seen in South Africa [2] :—

> "The evolution of the Indian from a newly-arrived lascar practically penniless to a trader owning one or more shops, is interesting to consider. Sleeping on boxes in the proportion, perhaps, of a dozen in one room, and able to subsist on little other than a small quantity of

[1] *South African Trade Journal*, June 2, 1906.
[2] Ibid.

rice daily, he is able to save a considerable portion of the profit he earns from the hawking of fruit. In two years' time or less, he has saved some £50 or so. He hires a small room from a shop, at say £3 to £4 per month. By paying half cash he obtains goods to the value of his total capital from one firm of merchants, and on the strength of the invoices he obtains credit from others to a like amount. His trade is chiefly cash, and before long he is able to take 75 days' credit and then 90 days; and by the end of two or three years he may have several shops open. His orders are now considerable, and he is able to command prices from the merchant which would surprise the smaller white trader.

"Combination among the latter class to prevent ruinous cutting of prices means playing into the hands of the Indian.

"If a merchant, feeling uneasy at the largeness of an Indian's outstanding account, curtails supplies, his customer distributes his orders among other merchants, and in reply to the merchant's inquiries, says he is better suited elsewhere. Probably the matter ends in the Indian getting even better terms than before from the merchant. Should the merchant require a guarantee, another Indian is easily forthcoming, and the man he thus obliges guarantees him with other firms.

"The outset of his career in the country has thus been marked by a method of living which is a danger to the health of the community, not merely through the dirt and overcrowding in the rooms where he herds for the night with his fellows, but through the distribution among the inhabitants of fruit which has not merely been handled by him, but frequently has passed the night in those same surroundings.

"As a trader, he is able to compete with the respectable white shopkeeper with overwhelming advantages on his side.

"To an assistant he will pay from £1 to £2 per month, he himself can live on comparatively a few shillings a month, and he will keep open perhaps nineteen hours out of the twenty-four. He systematically infringes the Sunday Closing Act and the Half-Holiday Act, and not infrequently evades the latter measure by hawking from door to door.

"Against such methods as these, competition on the part of the respectable white trader is rendered impossible. Even the coloured shopkeeper has been driven to the wall, a loss resulting, *inter alia,* to the larger shopkeeper, who, to no inconsiderable extent, played towards him the rôle of wholesale man.

"It is probably not far off the mark to say that the Indian, through his methods of living, his cheap assistance and so on, can do nearly twice as well as the white grocer on half the turnover."

At a recent meeting of the Worcester Chamber of Commerce it was stated that one Indian controlled twenty-nine shops in Capetown alone.

The figures given however do not relate solely to British-Indians. The registered Chinese population of the Cape Colony on December 31, 1905, was 1,300, of whom 1,088 lived in the following centres :

Capetown (including Wynberg), Port Elizabeth (including Uitenhage), Kimberley (including Beaconsfield), and East London. Their occupations [1] included the following :—

Occupation	Number
General dealers and shopkeepers	460
Laundry owners and assistants	345
Shop assistants	335
Bookkeepers and clerks	92
Gardeners	58
Cooks	33
Carpenters	20

There is not likely to be an increase in these figures. The Chinese Exclusion Act in the Cape has been in operation since 1904, and since the first registrations of Chinese there has been a decrease of ninety-three in the Chinese population of the colony.

In the Transvaal there is also at the moment some difficulty in gauging the extent of Asiatic competition, as the Census figures relating to occupations deal simply with "Coloured." In the days of the Republic, however, a petition from the British-Indians to the Marquis of Ripon stated that there were 200 traders, whose liquidated assets would amount to nearly £100,000. Three firms were declared to "import directly from England, Durban, Port Elizabeth, India and other places." There may be fewer Indian traders to-day than before the war, but the general impression is that they do more of the trade of the colony than was formerly the case.

[1] Cape Immigration Report, 1905.

In 1905 the number of general dealers' *businesses* existing in Johannesburg was as follows :—

Europeans	3,484
Indian	270
Chinese	255
	4,009

Sometimes, however, more licences are granted than there are businesses.

In recent years the number of Asiatic *licences issued* in the Johannesburg district have been :—

	Total licences.	Asiatics.	Percentage of Asiatics.
1904 . .	3,799	535	14·13
1903 . .	3,418	397	11·61

In addition the Municipality of Johannesburg issued in 1905 the following licences to Asiatics as distinct from general dealers' licences :—

Description.	Number Dec. 31, 1903.	Number Dec. 31, 1904.	Number Nov. 28, 1905.
Hawkers	1,684	1,438	1,202
Bakers	—	—	2
Butchers	—	40	33
Kaffir eating-houses .	—	9	3
Dairies	—	—	3
Laundries	—	—	44
Restaurants	—	—	6
Totals . . .	1,684	1,487	1,293

This table is interesting as corroborating Mr. Evans' remarks as to the tendency of the Indians in Natal to enter a higher business grade. The hawker of to-day is the storekeeper of to-morrow. The fall in the number of licences issued in Johannesburg between the dates given—391 less—is probably due to the fact that there has been a migration to the small country towns away from the Golden City.

There has undoubtedly been a good deal of misapprehension concerning the number of Asiatics in the Transvaal to-day. During his recent tour Lord Selborne was assured by deputation after deputation that the influx was still proceeding. He gave emphatic assurances that this was not the case, and inquiries made go to show that the total is probably less than in the pre-war days. The figures given of the number of Asiatic stores in the country towns have also been exaggerated. But the latest statistics, obtained in March, 1906, by the Transvaal representative of *Indian Opinion* (and still uncontradicted), give :—

BRITISH-INDIAN TRADERS.

	Before the War.	To-day.
Pietersburg . . .	23	35
Potchefstroom . .	22	19

Indian Opinion offered to give the names of the traders and forfeit £50 if the figures were wrong.

Yet at a public meeting in June, 1906, at Krugersdorp a speaker declared the figures were :—

	Before the War.	To-day.
Pietersburg . . .	14	49
Potchefstroom . .	12	64

It may be that in the latter figures the big districts of which these towns are the headquarters, and not the towns themselves, have been taken; but this does not explain the discrepancy before the war. But taking the smaller figures as correct, they do not get rid of the statement made at the Transvaal National Convention of Asiatics that thirteen or fourteen European stores in Potchefstroom, and many more in other country towns, had been compelled to close down owing to this competition. The Post Office reports also afford indirect evidence that the Asiatics in the Transvaal are doing well, for from October 1, 1903, to October 1, 1904, a sum of £118,859 was remitted to India in postal orders alone from Johannesburg, Pretoria, Pietersburg and Potchefstroom. Sometimes charges are made against the Indian traders of dishonest practices and suspicious insolvencies. These, however, are not substantiated, and should not receive credence. The greatest compliment to the upright dealings of the Indians is the fact, admitted publicly both in Pretoria and Durban, that the Indian can get credit from the wholesale firms when white traders are refused. Naturally this does not increase the love of the white trader for his Asiatic rival.

That Asiatic competition is a serious factor in the commercial life of the smaller towns of the Transvaal is clear from the amount of feeling the question arouses. In some cases Vigilance Associations have been formed, largely to watch the Asiatic traders. Public meetings have been held at which resolutions have been passed demanding the removal of the Asiatics to locations. In one case a boycott was resolved upon, and pickets were placed before the Indian stores to see who purchased at them; at another place a "black list" was drawn up of all property owners who had let premises to Indian traders—who, by the way, usually offer higher rents than Europeans. The latest idea was embodied in the following resolution carried by the Krugersdorp Town Council :—

> (*a*) "That in future no tender for Municipal work or supplies be accepted from any person, persons or company, hiring or leasing business premises to Asiatics. (*b*) That notice of motion be given to the Transvaal Municipal Association : That legislation be enacted at the earliest possible date, vesting in local authorities the allocation of trading stands and residential premises to Asiatics.

CHAPTER V

BRITISH INDIANS IN THE TRANSVAAL

"In all the towns of the Transvaal the Asiatic question overshadows all others, and I fear that unless we are able to reconcile the opinion in England with the opinion held in this country the Government will be landed in a serious deadlock."—Sir ARTHUR LAWLEY, Lieut.-Governor of the Transvaal, 1904.

IN the immediate future one is more likely to hear of a particular phase of the Asiatic problem in the Colonies than of the general question. The discussion which must inevitably arise concerning the status of the British-Indians in the Transvaal may result in the establishment of a precedent according to which other colonies will be expected to model their laws. But a satisfactory solution appears impossible. To meet the claims of the Indians would involve the overruling of Colonial opinion ; to consent to the enactments of a local legislature would call forth loud protests against injustice from the Indian community. The difficulties are increased by the promises made by the English Government in the days before the war, and by what was at least believed to be the voice of the British population in the Republic. Whatever may have been said before the war, it is clear that British opinion in the Transvaal to-day is even more opposed to the British-Indian trader than was the policy of the Dutch. The Boer farmer wishes to buy cheaply, and, as students of the debates in the old Volksraad will see, the country view is that "the European storekeepers charged poor people very high prices for the staff of life, while the coolies charged much less." [1] Broadly speaking, however, Sir Arthur Lawley was perfectly right when he wrote in 1904: "The Asiatic question overshadows all others." It is a subject on which—like the native question—the Colonists would certainly resent interference from England. Yet the last word must lie with the Imperial Government. "Unfortunately," said an official in the Transvaal Legislative Council three years ago, "the question of the status of the Asiatic is not a local one capable of settlement by local legislation." Lord Milner elaborated the point when replying to a deputation on the subject of the Constitution.[2] He said:—

> "There is one restriction which always exists in any colony, whether it be a colony under Crown Colony Government or with representative institutions, or with full self-government. That is, of course, the ultimate power of the Crown to veto any measure. That would no doubt continue. It is universal, and I should like attention to one point for the illumination of the public, who seem to be suffering from

[1] *Proceedings in the Volksraad*, November 4, 1896.

[2] January 10, 1905.

extraordinary delusion with regard to it: and that is that the power of veto resting in the Crown is absolutely the same whether you have Responsible Government or whether you have Representative Government. You do not get rid of the veto by having Responsible Government. You do not increase the veto by having Representative Government. I say this especially with regard to such questions as native affairs or Asiatic affairs. . . . If a measure was to be passed here dealing either with Asiatic affairs or with native affairs which, whether the Home Government approved of it or not, appeared to it to be a measure which infringed the right of British subjects and which therefore the Home Government ought to veto, it would equally veto it under Responsible Government. As far as dealing with native affairs or Asiatic affairs is concerned, you will have exactly the same powers under the one system as under the other."

The question, however, stands somewhat apart from the general principle of Asiatic immigration, or even of the restrictions which may be placed on British-Indian subjects. Hitherto the problem has been considered on the broadest lines. The Indian coolies in Natal happen to be British subjects; but they might have been Chinese-British subjects from Hong Kong. The British-Indians in the Transvaal are, so to speak, more than British subjects. Special interest was taken in their case in the old days of

Krugerism, special protests were raised on their behalf, special pledges were given. The general objection to Asiatic immigration applies to them ; but it must be modified by the peculiar circumstances of the case. The controversy has been a long one, yet it needs to be studied to understand why principles which can be applied to newcomers from India cannot honestly be said to govern this particular and exceptional instance.

Article XIV of the London Convention of 1884 provided that all persons, other than natives, conforming themselves to the laws of the South African Republic—

> (*a*) Will have full liberty, with their families, to enter, travel, or reside in any part of the South African Republic.
>
> (*b*) Will be entitled to hire or possess houses, manufactories, warehouses, shops and premises.
>
> (*c*) May carry on their commerce either in person or by any agents whom they may think fit to employ.

Indian traders had entered the Republic some three years before this, and their increasing number directed attention to their presence—" they aroused the jealousy of white traders, and soon there sprang up an anti-Indian agitation, initiated by Chambers of Commerce wherein the British element was predominant." [1] The Republic attempted to enforce restrictive regulations, and the Indians, as British

[1] *Statement of the British-Indian Community to the Transvaal Constitution Committee* (*see* Appendix I).

subjects, appealed to the English Government against what they claimed was a violation of Article XIV of the London Convention.

The Volksraad passed Law 3 of 1885, of which the world has heard much. This applied to "the persons belonging to one of the aboriginal races of Asia," and prohibited them from being owners of landed property, also stipulating that those who entered the country should pay a registration fee, and that the Government should have the right to point out to them their proper streets, wards, and locations *for residence* ("ter bewoning"). The Republic proposed to apply this law to what were known as the "Arab" traders and to coolies indiscriminately; and the British-Indians approached the Imperial Government. After some correspondence a Proclamation was issued from Pretoria modifying the law by inserting the words "for sanitary purposes." The Republic, however, still wished to bring the higher class Asiatics within the scope of the measure, and also claimed that the term "for residence" meant that the Asiatics could be compelled not merely to *reside* in but to *trade* in places set apart for them. Eventually the matter was referred to arbitration, and the Chief Justice of the Orange River Colony set aside both claims, and ruled that the interpretation of Law 3 of 1885 rested with the ordinary tribunals of the country. Ultimately a test case was taken before the Supreme Court of the Republic, and by two to one the judges decided that the words "ter bewoning" covered a merchant's place of business. The way was thus clear for removing all the Asiatic traders to locations. The law, however, was not enforced, the explanation offered in the Volksraad being that if the Executive fixed a location in one place, "the coolies would flock to the place where there was none." [1] Much was heard on both sides. One petition against the Indians alluded to "the dangers to which the whole community is exposed by the spread of leprosy, syphilis and the like loathsome diseases, engendered by the filthy habits and immoral practices of these people." [2] In a memorial presented to the Volksraad of the Orange River Colony, a copy of which the Pretoria Chamber of Commerce sent with approval to the Transvaal Government, was the following passage: "As these men enter the State without wives or female relatives the result is obvious. Their religion teaches them to consider all women as soulless and Christians as natural prey." On the other hand, a Dutch petition, signed by 484 burghers, stated that the withdrawal of the traders would be a hardship; and another, signed by 1,340 Europeans, declared that the sanitary habits of the Indians were equal to Europeans, and that the agitation was due to trade jealousy.

Unfortunately the complaints of the Indians were used for political purposes. It may be that the opinion of the Transvaal was misrepresented in England; it may be that in the heat of a great struggle the Uitlanders made use of weapons without very closely examining their real effect. But

[1] *Volksraad Debate*, November 3, 1896.

[2] *Transvaal Green Book*, No. 2, pp. 19–21.

certain it is that words were used and promises made which do not coincide with the opinion of the Transvaal to-day. This is not the place to discuss the controversies which led to the war. All that needs to be remembered is that the real feeling of the white population in the Transvaal did not justify the tenor of some of the utterances of English statesmen. At Sheffield in 1899 Lord Lansdowne said :—

> "Among the many misdeeds of the South African Republic I do not know that any fills me with more indignation than its treatment of these Indians. And the harm is not confined to the sufferers on the spot ; for what do you imagine would be the effect produced in India when these poor people return to their country to report to their friends that the Government of the Empress, so mighty and irresistible in India, with its population of 300,000,000, is powerless to secure redress at the hands of a small South African State ?"

From Press and platform came many similar expressions. As Sir M. M. Bhownaggree said in the remarkably able statement of the Indian claims he submitted to the Colonial Secretary a few years ago : "Those of us who are specially interested in this subject were led by the assurances of Cabinet Ministers to cherish the anticipation that the war had for one of its main objects the rescue of British-Indians from the harsh treatment to which they were exposed by the late Boer Republics."

But to-day the Indian community complain that they are more harshly treated than in the days of Paul Kruger's rule. One thing, however, was decided in their favour. A case was brought before the Transvaal Supreme Court to see whether the words "ter bewoning" in Law 3 of 1885 meant for residence only or included for business purposes. The decision of the Boer Court was reversed, and thus it followed, to quote one of Mr. Alfred Lyttelton's despatches, "that every Asiatic now resident in the Transvaal (except those brought in under indenture under a special Ordinance) is as free to carry on trade where he pleases as is a subject of English or Dutch origin." This decision led the Home Government to refuse to sanction certain location proposals put forward by the Transvaal Legislative Council, and lately the subject, like others, has been set aside to be dealt with by Responsible Government.

Morally and logically the Indians have a very strong case. Vested interests have been acquired under the protection of the British Government. The indignation of that Government at the slightest hint of hardship or oppression to its humblest subjects moved the world to admiration. The Indians had every reason to believe that after the war the grievances upon which the support of the Home Government had been received would be instantly removed. The grievances still remain. Is it to be wondered at that the Indians cannot now resist the temptation of asking what will be the "effect produced in India" when they return and report that, having now the power to redress the complaints which filled Lord Lansdowne with such indignation, the Government of the King-Emperor does nothing at all—or rather, enforces harsh laws which the Boer Republic, under our pressure allowed to remain in abeyance? They point to the burden of Empire which the poor Indian peoples support, and ask what does South Africa, with all its gold and diamonds, contribute compared to the millions demanded annually from the despised "coolies," who are not deemed fit to walk on a pavement or ride on a tram?

But the Transvaal does not attempt to argue with the subtle-minded educated Indian on these points. It pins itself stubbornly to the tale of white traders driven out of the small towns by Asiatic competition, and echoes Sir Arthur Lawley's reply to the revived pledges: "If the redemption of the pledges upon which Sir M. M. Bhownaggree depends both in letter and in spirit means that in fifty or a hundred years this country will have fallen to the inheritance of Eastern instead of Western populations, then from the point of view of civilization they must be numbered among promises which it is a greater crime to keep than to break." A very convenient reply to many things—but what if Mr. Kruger had used it?

The British-Indians cry out that if the Dutch scourged them with whips, the British scourge them with scorpions. Since the establishment of British rule, laws which in the old days were allowed to fall into abeyance have been enforced. In the case of Nabob Motan *v.* The Transvaal Government, in the

Transvaal Supreme Court in May, 1904, by which it was ruled that it was illegal for revenue officers to refuse to grant trading licences to Asiatics for premises situated in any part of the town, the Chief Justice, Sir James Rose-Innes, said :—

> "It does strike one as remarkable that, without fresh legislation, the officials of the Crown in the Transvaal should put forward a claim which the Government of the Crown in England has always contended was illegal under the statute, and which in the past it has strenuously resisted."

But whatever was said in England, and whatever was the language of the petitions signed in the Transvaal—the organizing of petitions has become a fine art in the Transvaal—there can be no doubt that the great mass of Colonial opinion is dead against the Asiatic. The National Convention on Asiatics held in the Opera House, Pretoria, in November, 1904, was one of the most representative gatherings ever witnessed in the Transvaal. It was attended by 160 delegates of Municipalities, Chambers of Commerce, Agricultural Societies, Farmers' Associations, Ratepayers' Associations, the Witwatersrand Trade and Labour Council, etc. The resolutions were as follows :—

> 1. "That in the opinion of this Convention the serious delay that has occurred in dealing with the question of the status of the Asiatics has been and is highly prejudicial to the best

interests of the Transvaal, and increases the difficulty of arriving at a satisfactory settlement.

2. "That having regard to the enormous preponderance of the native races in this country, the difficulties surrounding the settlement of native policy, and the necessity for protecting the existing European population and encouraging further European immigration, this Convention affirms the principle that Asiatic immigration should be prohibited except under the provisions of the Labour Importation Ordinance."

(*Note.*—The original resolution moved was "except under restrictive legislation." The more drastic amendment, however, was carried, only a dozen or so opposing.)

3. "That this Convention having regard to the importance of arriving at a permanent and conclusive settlement of the whole question and of preventing any further attempts to reopen the matter, urges upon the Government the advisability of removing into bazaars all Asiatic traders, compensation being provided for such as may have vested interests which have been legally acquired."

(*Note.*—An attempt was made to do away with the reference to compensation.)

4. "That this Convention, recognizing the grave danger resulting from the continued issue of trading licences to Asiatics permitting trade outside bazaars, requests the Government to

take immediate steps to pass the necessary legal enactments to prevent any further issue of such licences."

5. "That with regard to the appointment of any proposed Commission to deal with the Asiatic question, this Convention urges upon the Government the necessity for including therein men other than officials, with a thorough knowledge of existing conditions in South Africa."

6. "That this Convention affirms its opinion that all Asiatics should be required to reside in bazaars."

The spirit of the National Convention was shown by the voting in the last resolution. Originally it read "subject only to exemptions made in accordance with the last paragraph of *Government Notice*, No. 356, of 1903, viz.: With regard to the residence of Asiatics, which by the law above mentioned is confined to those streets, wards and locations which may be set apart for the purpose, His Excellency has decided that an exception shall be made in favour of those whose intellectual attainments, or social qualities and habits of life, appear to entitle them to it, and has accordingly resolved that any Asiatic who shall prove to the satisfaction of the Colonial Secretary that he holds any higher educational certificate from the Educational Department in this or any other British Colony or Dependency, or that he is able and willing to adopt a mode of living not repugnant to European ideas nor in conflict with sanitary laws, may apply to the Colonial Secretary for a letter of exemption which shall enable him to reside elsewhere than in a place especially set apart for Asiatics."

But the Convention threw out the exemption clause, and thus bound itself down to the principle that an educated British-Indian, even if he happened to be a member of the House of Commons, or a Prince deemed socially worthy of entertaining the future King and Queen of England, should be forced to reside in a location with the Madrassi waiters from a railway restaurant or the Bombay hawker from the gateway of a mine compound.

More moderate but sufficiently drastic are the principles laid down by the Transvaal Progressive Association, which claims to have 40,000 members. Its recent manifesto included the following :—

> "The following questions affecting Asiatics have been considered :—
>
> "Immigration restriction,
>
> "Trading licences,
>
> "Residence in bazaars,
>
> "Regulation of travelling by railway ;
>
> "and the following are the recommendations adopted :—
>
> (1) IMMIGRATION RESTRICTIONS.
>
> "It is desirable that the immigration of Asiatics into the Transvaal should be absolutely prohibited except in the case of indentured labourers who are subject to repatriation on the expiration of the terms of their contracts,

and to the other provisions of the Labour Importation Ordinance, power being reserved to the Colonial Secretary to grant exemption to individuals under special and exceptional circumstances. At the same time the practical impossibility of passing into law a prohibitive measure framed on the above lines, and specially directed against Asiatics, is recognized.

"It is therefore recommended: That a general Immigration Ordinance be passed in the Transvaal, framed on the lines of those in force in other Colonies.

(2) TRADING LICENCES.

(*a*) "That the issue of new trading licences to Asiatics, entitling the holders to trade outside bazaars, be prohibited by legislation, but that Asiatics who held such licences prior to the war be allowed to renew the same in respect of existing establishments, but be not allowed to transfer such licences to other Asiatics.

(*b*) "That municipal authorities be empowered to require the removal to bazaars of Asiatics who are trading within their area outside bazaars, subject to such authorities undertaking the payment of compensation for vested interests.

(*c*) "That full power be given to municipal authorities to control the issue of licences to Asiatic hawkers within their districts, and to regulate such hawkers.

(3) Residence in Bazaars.

(*a*) "That all Asiatics be required to reside in bazaars or other localities appointed by the Government, with the exception of Asiatics holding letters of exemption.

(*b*) "That the Colonial Secretary be authorized to grant a letter of exemption to any Asiatic who shall prove to the satisfaction of the Colonial Secretary that his status and mode of life entitle him to such exemption.

(4) Regulation of Travelling by Railway.

"That Asiatics be provided with such accommodation on the railways as they are prepared to pay for, but that such accommodation be separate from that which is provided for white persons."

These regulations form a minimum restrictive policy which would satisfy the bulk of the white population.

Now what do the Indians claim? [1] Generally they ask for equal rights with the white inhabitants so far as trading, residence and locomotion are concerned. That is to say, they want all the civic rights as distinguished from the social and political. They recognize that the white man must dominate the sub-continent, but they object to be placed on a level with the Kaffir. In particular they claim :—

[1] A full statement of the British-Indian claims will be found in Appendix I.

The right to reside in any part of the colony, subject to strict municipal supervision and the ordinary municipal bye-laws.

The right to receive licences to trade, subject to control by the local bodies, so that over-trading may be avoided, and those who may not conform to the habits of the predominant race may be largely prevented from trading.

The right to own landed property in any part of the country.

The right to move about freely, that is, the usual facilities for the use of public conveyances in common with the white inhabitants.

In other words, the Indians claim the repeal of all class legislation so far as they are concerned, and therefore of the anti-Asiatic law of 1885, Lord Milner's bazaar notice, the laws relating to the use of footpaths, etc. They contend that for a law-abiding people, as the Indians are admitted to be, the ordinary laws of the country provide ample safeguards against abuses. The charges of dirtiness and of non-compliance with ordinary sanitary rules —which they do not admit—could be enforced by the strict carrying out of the existing laws; in fact, there would be no objection to locations for coolies if a wide exemption clause was permitted. The great bugbear to the Colonial is the Indian trader, but the Indians claim that the case will be fully met if they consent to the control of licences being given to the usual local bodies, subject, in exceptional cases, to review by the Supreme Court—an important modification of the Natal law.

Existing licences must be scrupulously respected, but even here exceptions could be made in cases in which the licence-holders do not keep decent stores separate from their lodgings, and do not have their books kept in the English language. The latter point meets the objection of some white firms, that the books of the Indian traders cannot be understood by any judge, and that a loophole is thus provided for ingenious frauds at the expense of wholesale firms. On the question of the owning of land, too, the Indians would agree to a clause against speculative dealing.

But however reasonable these claims may seem to the Home public, the colonists are not to-day prepared to concede them. The British-Indian problem in the Transvaal is indeed one of special difficulty. The pledges of the past cannot be calmly thrown aside. How strongly the conditions of to-day are resented in India is shown by the fact that the Government of India refused to allow the Transvaal to recruit 10,000 coolies to work on the railways, "while the position of the British-Indian traders resident in the Transvaal remained in so unsatisfactory a state." How this problem might be solved, as part of a general policy towards Asiatic immigration, is suggested in another chapter.

CHAPTER VI

THE CASE OF AUSTRALASIA

"Cabinet Ministers recognize difficulties as to Australian complications and reasonable grounds for Chinese attitude, and as loyal subjects of Queen of England, do not wish to embarrass, but question of Chinese immigration has an irresistible disturbing force which they fear that those who are not on the spot cannot adequately appreciate."—Telegram from Lord CARRINGTON (New South Wales) to Lord KNUTSFORD (Colonial Secretary), June 12, 1888.

ALTHOUGH—perhaps because—Australia has practically no native population which counts in the labour market, the Colonies have as a rule been strongly opposed to the introduction of Asiatics. Taking the Great South Land as a whole, there has never grown up that spirit of helplessness without cheap coloured labour which is so characteristic of South Africa. The need for workers has been as great as in other countries, the temptation to obtain a supply at the expense of the future of the continent has been ever present. At some periods there were signs of wavering. The squatters in the north, feeling the pinch of an ill-supplied labour market, were eager to secure any one—Polynesians, Indians, Chinese, Japanese, or even English convicts. In

Queensland Sir Samuel Griffiths, who had long opposed indentured labour, changed his policy, and the introduction of the Kanakas was followed by a distinct revival in material prosperity. The ending of the experiment was opposed in the territory concerned, and no doubt the estates would be more prosperous to-day could the islanders be obtained as freely as in the past. Other districts had their advocates of imported labour, and it is interesting to remember that Sir Henry Parkes, subsequently the most vigorous opponent of the whole system, once sent to Madras for Eurasian compositors to set up his *Empire* newspaper. Experiments with Asiatics were tried in various places, but did not prove strikingly successful, and the bulk of the population was decidedly opposed to this form of immigration. As far back as 1854, Sir Charles Hotham, the second Governor of Victoria, after a tour round the goldfields, reported to the Home Government that he thought the introduction of Chinese into the colony undesirable. The mines, however, attracted an increasing number of Chinese, and gradually legislation of a drastic character was adopted. The favourite restrictive method was a poll tax of £10 and a law that only one Chinese should be brought by any ship for every 100 tons of registered tonnage. The influx, however, was considerable, and twenty years ago a great battle was fought over Chinese immigration, during which certain principles were laid down which it is well to remember to-day.

In the years 1886–7 the Chinese Government displayed considerable activity in protesting against the Colonial enactments which had been passed against its subjects. In July, 1886, a long letter of complaint was addressed to Lord Rosebery regarding the Chinese Regulation Act of 1884 in British Columbia, in which it was alleged in the preamble that the Chinese "are not disposed to be governed by our laws, are dissimilar in habits and occupation from our people, evade the payment of taxes justly due to the Government, are governed by pestilential habits, are useless in cases of emergency, habitually desecrate graveyards by the removal of bodies therefrom, and generally the laws governing the whites are found to be inapplicable to the Chinese, and such Chinese are inclined to habits subversive to the comfort and well-being of the community." Lew Ta Jen claimed that "it would be contrary to international usage to make them (the Chinese) the subject of an invidious legislation, or to impose on them burthens from which the inhabitants of the country, and more especially other foreigners following the same vocations, are exempt."

Chinese Commissioners had visited the Australian Colonies to inquire into "the condition of Chinese subjects residing in these parts of Her Britannic Majesty's Dominions." The correspondence which followed[1] contains very clear statements of both sides of the case, and as the arguments are applicable to Asiatic immigration generally, the main points may be quoted.

[1] Correspondence relating to Chinese immigration into the Australian Colonies, 1888 (c. 5448).

In the first note to the English Government the Chinese Minister in London remarked :—

> " In the Crown Colonies it has not been found necessary to treat Chinese subjects differently from the subjects of other Powers, and it is difficult to understand why it should be otherwise in those Colonies to whom a certain amount of self-government has been conferred. It has never been alleged that Chinese immigrants were unruly. For, not only in Hong Kong and the Straits Settlements, but also in Australia, the Colonial Governors have repeatedly borne testimony to the orderly conduct of the Chinese population, and to their value in developing the Colonial resources. There does not, therefore, appear to be any sufficient reason for their being deprived of the immunities accorded to them by the treaties and the law of nations, or to their being treated differently from the subjects of other Powers residing in the same parts of Her Britannic Majesty's Dominions."

The different methods adopted by Crown Colonies and those with a certain " amount of self-government," arose, of course, from the varying proportion of white people due to climatic influences. The Crown Colonies consist in the main of tropical areas in which there is no room for any considerable white population, and yet in which the demand for labour is great. The very fact that other colonies had received a measure of self-government indicated that there was a growing white population, which in its turn presupposed a more temperate climate and room for additional Europeans. From the Chinese standpoint the case was admirably stated by Lew Ta Jen. But his argument was based upon the principle that Chinese immigration is on the same footing as any other immigration and must be governed by the same laws. As the Colonies would not accept these premises, there was never any approach to agreement, and the dispute raged for months. Popular feeling in Australia was raised to fever heat by the " Chinese scare " which sprang up. The Government Resident at Port Darwin in South Australia notified to the Government at Adelaide that large vessels flying the Chinese flag and freighted with Chinese labour to work the ruby mines were approaching his district by way of North Australia. The result was panic legislation, Sir Henry Parkes rushing his Chinese Restriction Bill through the New South Wales Assembly in a day and the authorities refusing to permit Chinese immigrants to land. The Supreme Court decided against the authorities and eventually the legislation was modified; but whilst the agitation lasted some very strong language was used, and the whole controversy showed what great importance is attached to the question in the Australian Colonies. The arguments employed by these colonies are applicable to-day.

On behalf of New South Wales, which had more Chinese than the other colonies, Lord Carrington advanced seven reasons for restricting Chinese immigration. He wrote on April 2, 1888 :—

"We desire . . . to impress upon Her Majesty's Imperial advisers the more prominent phases of the Chinese question as it specially and almost exclusively affects the Australian section of the British people : firstly, the Australian ports are within easy sail of the ports of China ; secondly, the climate, as well as certain branches of trade and industry in Australia, such as the cultivation of the soil for domestic purposes, and tin and gold mining, are peculiarly attractive to the Chinese ; thirdly, the working classes of the British people in all the affinities of race are directly opposed to their Chinese competitors ; fourthly, there can be no sympathy, and in the future it is to be apprehended that there will be no peace, between the two races ; fifthly, the enormous number of the Chinese population intensifies every consideration of this class of immigration in comparison with the immigration of any other nation ; sixthly, the most prevailing determination in all the Australian communities is to preserve the British type in the population ; seventhly, there can be no interchange of ideas of religion or citizenship, nor can there be intermarriage or social communion between the British and the Chinese. It is respectfully submitted that the examination of these principal phases of the question can only lead to one conclusion, namely, that the Chinese must be restricted from emigrating to any part of Australasia."

In a memorandum submitted on behalf of the Colony of Victoria—where the Chinese increased from 2,000 in 1854 to 42,000 in 1859—stress is laid on another side of the question :—

> "Members of the European family of nations forming our community become amalgamated with the general population ; they bring their wives and children with them ; their habits of life, their style of civilization, their religion and morals, and their physique are so much in an equality with our own that they blend readily with the population and are heartily welcome.
>
> "The Chinese stand out in marked contrast. They come without their women and children, apparently having no intention to settle, and occupy an isolated position in every community where they are found ; the 'Chinese quarter' in our cities and principal towns is proverbial ; it is always distinct and often notorious.
>
> "Nor is it the mere fact of this isolation, but the impossibility of its being otherwise.
>
> "The Chinese, from all points of view, are so entirely dissimilar as to render a blending of the peoples out of the question.
>
> "They are not only of an alien race, but they remain aliens. Thus we have not a colonization in any true sense of the word, but practically a sort of peaceful invasion of our land by Chinese."

These views were generally approved in Australasia. The feeling in Northern Queensland in favour of Kanaka labour, and the desire expressed in parts of Western Australia for Chinese, carried little weight with the mass of the colonists. The majority were anti-Chinese. The Australasian Conference which sat at Sydney in June, 1888, comprised representatives from New South Wales, South Australia, Victoria, Queensland, Tasmania, and Western Australia. The following resolutions were carried :—

1. "That in the opinion of this Conference the further restriction of Chinese immigration is essential to the welfare of the people of Australasia.

2. "That this Conference is of opinion that the desired restriction can best be secured through the diplomatic action of the Imperial Government and by uniform Australasian legislation.

3. "That this Conference resolves to consider a joint representation to the Imperial Government for the purpose of obtaining the desired diplomatic action.

4. "That this Conference is of opinion that the desired Australasian legislation should contain the following provisions :—

(*a*) "That it shall apply to all Chinese, with specified restrictions.

(*b*) "That the restriction should be by limitation of the number of Chinese which any vessel may bring into any Australian port to one passenger to every 500 tons of the ship's burthen.

(*c*) "That the passage of Chinese from one Colony to another without consent of the Colony which they enter be made a misdemeanour."

Tasmania dissented to the first and fourth resolutions and Western Australia did not vote on them. The second and third, however, were carried unanimously.

"In so serious a crisis," read the concluding paragraph of Lord Carrington's official report of the Conference, "the Colonial Governments have felt called upon to take strong and decisive action to protect their peoples; but in doing so they have been studious of Imperial interests, of international obligations, and of their reputation as law-abiding communities. They now confidently rely upon the support and assistance of Her Majesty's Government in their endeavour to prevent their country from being overrun by an alien race, who are incapable of assimilation in the body politic, strangers to our civilization, out of sympathy with our aspirations, and unfitted for our free institutions, to which their presence in any number would be a source of constant danger."

The keenness of the alarm of the moment, and the strength of the feeling that this was a matter for the Colonies to decide, are shown by two incidents. In May, 1888, the New Zealand Government republished proclamations declaring that strict quarantine would be enforced in reference to all vessels arriving from the places mentioned or having "received any person or thing whatsoever from or out of any vessel coming from or having touched at any of such places." These proclamations declared that:—

1. "The Empire of China and the British Posses-

sion of Hong Kong are infected with the disease called smallpox.

2. "The Island of Sumatra is infected with the disease called cholera.

3. "The Island of Java and the Islands of the Eastern Archipelago are infected with the disease called cholera, and that Mauritius is infected with the disease called smallpox."

And Sir Henry Parkes, speaking on the Chinese Restriction Bill, 1888, in the New South Wales Legislative Assembly, put the case for Australia as strongly as any one could: "In this crisis" (he said) "of the Chinese question, and it is a crisis, we have acted calmly with a desire to see clearly the way before us; but at the same time we have acted with decision and we don't mean to turn back. Neither for Her Majesty's ships of war, nor for Her Majesty's representative on the spot, nor for the Secretary of State for the Colonies, do we intend to turn aside from our purpose, which is to terminate the landing of Chinese on these shores for ever, except under the restrictions imposed by the Bill, which will amount, and which are intended to amount, to practical prohibition."

Yet whether the tropical part of Queensland would have become more prosperous, and whether it would ultimately have become of greater or less value to the Great South Land had there been an uninterrupted supply of cheap Asiatic labour, must remain a matter for controversy. It is argued that even here white men can do the rough work. Sir Henry Parkes, in his autobiography, recollects Sir

Samuel Griffiths replying to the argument that white men could not do the unskilled labour in this part of the continent by interposing sharply, " Who says they can't do it ?—I say they can ! "[1] But it was Sir Samuel Griffiths who eventually consented to import coloured labour—a change of policy which was followed by a marked revival in the prosperity of that part of the colony.

It may be that the determination of Australia not to import cheap Asiatic labour has retarded development. Probably less land is cultivated than would have been had the policy of Natal been followed ; perhaps industries would have developed faster. But it must also be remembered that Australia has shown a tendency to adopt a selfish attitude towards white immigrants. The inducements which have drawn hundreds of thousands to Canada have been withheld. There has often been evidence of a desire to limit the influx even of an English population. But there is a change to-day. Within the past two years Australia has begun to realize that, unless she possesses a numerically strong white population, she may in some distant period fall a prey to the growing Asiatic Powers at her gate. The old selfish policy will be abandoned. And now that there is this wish for more white men there must be a sense of gratitude to those who fought the battle in the eighties and determined that the vacant spaces should not be filled up by an alien race. At least Australia deserves praise for having acted up to the ideal of a White Man's Country.

[1] See Preface.

CHAPTER VII

SOME OF THE DANGERS

". . . If the unnaturalized Chinese should at any time become as numerous, or nearly as numerous, in any colony, as the residents of European origin, the result would be either an attempt on the part of the Chinese to establish separate institutions of a character which would trench on the supremacy of the present legislative and administrative authorities, or a tacit acceptance by them of an inferior social and political position which, associated with the avocations that the majority of them would probably follow, would create a combined political and industrial division of society upon the basis of racial distinction. This would inevitably produce in the majority of the remainder of the population a degraded estimate of manual labour similar to that which has always existed in those communities where African slavery has been permitted, and thereby call into existence a class similar in habit and character to the 'mean whites' of the Southern States of the American Union before the Civil War. Societies so divided produce particular vices in exaggerated proportions, and are doomed to certain deterioration."—A. INGLIS CLARK, Attorney-General of Tasmania, 1888.

THAT Asiatic immigration on a large scale is a serious menace to the prosperity of a White Man's Country will probably be admitted. A greater degree of progress at the beginning of such an experiment does not prove that there is no ultimate danger. We may accept Darwin's theory that the prosperity of Australasia in the early days was directly due to convict labour, without pledging ourselves to support that system for all time. The labour of the Indians brought to Natal undoubtedly gave rise to a distinct forward movement in the tea and sugar industries, but this success does not imply that prosperity will continue to be attained in proportion to the number of indentured labourers imported. There comes a point at which a country must throw aside the crutch of contract labour or consent to be for ever crippled.

The danger in Australasia is clearly defined. The ideal of a White Man's Country has been adopted, and although progress of late years has been slow, that ideal is the best for the Colonies. A large influx of cheap coloured labour is inevitably ruinous to the white workman. There arises that prejudice which in South Africa will sometimes prevent a starving man from doing what he contemptuously calls "Kaffir's work." The white carpenter, the white mason, the white plumber, all insist upon having a native to carry their tool bag and do the roughest labour. With a big Chinese population in Australia the same system would spring up. The next stage would be that the Chinaman would become sufficiently expert to do the work, and the white man be compelled to join the ranks of the unemployed, or accept a Chinaman's wages and live down to a Chinaman's standard. It is useless to talk about education and the advance in the scale of civilization to a working class forced to compete with Asiatics. Free Asiatic immigration must inevitably mean a lower standard of living for the white working classes—if there is any chance of living at all.

But where there already exists a large native population the danger is intensified. There may eventually be reached the state of things which exists in Fiji,[1] where Indian coolies do the bulk of the work and the original inhabitants are being displaced and forced to emigrate.

In South Africa the danger of Asiatic immigration is peculiarly great, for it means not only decreased openings for white men, but also another obstacle placed in the way of the advancement of the native population. The native problem is the greatest question South Africa has to solve. In British South Africa the black population numbers 4,652,662, of whom 899,726 are males, between the ages of fifteen and forty. South of the Zambesi the natives number probably seven millions. In British South Africa this native population "has to derive its sustenance from a soil which is not everywhere fertile, and the native agriculturalist has to contend with the same drawbacks of drought and pestilence that beset the European farmer."[2] The native does not always waste his land. He is not invariably the lazy person he is generally supposed to be, even if his

[1] In June, 1906, there landed in Calcutta 350 returned emigrants from Fiji (including over 100 women and children). The men (less than 250 in number) brought Rs. 127,000 in savings, one man having Rs. 12,205—over £800.

[2] South African Native Affairs Commission's Report.

energies do not take the direction the white folk would like. In Natal over sixty per cent. of the natives—men and women—are breadwinners. Undoubtedly large tracts of land are not cultivated. But more of this land belongs to the European than to the native. The Kaffir, as travellers in South Africa notice, cultivates in patches. This does not arise from ignorance. The native's knowledge is empirical, but it is usually sound, and he does not walk an extra quarter of a mile because he wants exercise. The land is poor. In a Report by the Commissioner for Native Affairs relative to the acquisition and tenure of land by natives in the Transvaal (July, 1904), I find this statement :—

> "Nearly all the land suitable for agriculture and available for native purposes has already been taken up. There is therefore but little arable ground in reserve for the expanding and surplus native population unless artificial means of irrigation are employed."

In Natal, according to an official publication, "the ordinary Crown lands of the Colony are not suitable for settlement by newcomers." The South African Native Affairs Commission recommended that the purchase of land by natives should in future be limited to certain areas to be defined by legislative enactment, but the Natal delegates dissented, one of their reasons for doing so being this :—

> "That Asiatics and other coloured races not

> of African descent may purchase land anywhere, whereas by this resolution the natives, who are the aborigines of the country, will be excluded from this privilege except in limited areas selected, probably, for their unhealthiness and unsuitability for irrigation and cultivation and other kindred reasons."

What is to be the future of this huge native population if the land is to be filled up—as it is being filled up in Natal—by an ever increasing Indian population? The Garden Colony contains to-day 900,000 natives, where after the devastating wars of Dingiswayo, Chaka and Dingaan there were probably left not 10,000. This population grows rapidly—between 1891 and 1904 the increase was 33·45 per cent. In the great native areas the tribes are always growing bigger. True there is a shortage of unskilled labour. But this has been caused by the sudden upspringing of great industrial enterprises in a country where the native population is pastoral and agricultural. South Africa cannot live for ever on these industries. The life of the Rand itself, worked at the rate it is worked to-day (and the pace must be maintained owing to its financial obligations), is not unlimited, and when the Rand begins to be worked out the whole life of the sub-continent will be changed. In that day, when the native population will be far bigger, would it be well if large areas were in the hands of the Asiatics; if the unskilled labour on farm and in factory was performed by aliens? The native question in South

Africa is already sufficiently difficult without complicating it by having to deal with half a million or a million aliens from across the Indian Ocean, who will blend with no race. The recent trouble in one corner of Natal has shown South Africa what a tremendous task it would have if there was widespread discontent and rebellion between the Zambesi and the Southern Sea. For the satisfactory solution of the native problem it is better that the number of the Asiatics should be as small as possible; it is the white population which must be increased.

The manner in which the Asiatic competes with the European is obvious from the figures given. I know that it is claimed by the Indian community "that European progress can, in Natal at any rate, continue side by side with that of the Indian; indeed, may even be dependent upon the latter's progress."[1] But the undoubted prosperity of Natal is not altogether due to the Indian; the through traffic to the goldfields has had something to do with it. Admitting that the immigrants have enabled the colony to develop its industries and prosper, it is extremely doubtful whether that measure of prosperity will continue without serious disadvantages. The coolie is at once the salvation and the danger of Natal. Even the coast lands are not useful only to the Indian—many European fruit farmers and vegetable growers are still trying to gain a living there to-day despite the competition of the ex-indentured labourer. But granting that

[1] *Indian Opinion* (Durban), March 24, 1906.

100,000 Indians have done good service for Natal, what will be the effect of 300,000 or 600,000? The native trade which used to support many white families has almost gone; many industries are being encroached upon; in time the Indian clerk may be a feature of Natal business life. And yet in Natal to-day there are 31,500 white children under sixteen years of age. What is to be their future if the Indian works the farm, owns the store, and performs skilled labour in the factory? Already one finds in Natal newspaper advertisements requiring Indian engine drivers and Indian mechanics. Cheap labour is the demand, and the Indian steps into the place of the white man who cannot exist on such wages, and of the native who will not. On the Natal Railways last year there were employed 1,136 indentured Indians and 2,098 free Indians—more Indians than there are natives on the system. And in his report the General Manager remarked:—

> "Free Indian labour has been more plentiful, and this, together with the fact that the Immigration Department has been able to keep up a fairly good supply of Indentured men, has enabled the Department to reduce the rates of pay hitherto given to Free men."

The same tendency is found in agriculture. The openings for the white population are becoming more and more curtailed. How is it there are only 39 white cultivators to 3,031 Asiatics? And 103 white farm labourers to 16,142 Indians? And 39 European fruit farmers to 700 Asiatics similarly engaged? There are several reasons. There is the evil of absentee landlordism, by which men owning large areas live in England on the rents drawn from natives and Indians, and make no attempt to develop their estates for the benefit of the white population; there is the magnet of the Rand, which has drawn so much capital from Natal in the hope of quicker and larger profits; there is the old prejudice against manual labour in a land of blacks. These evils produce others. Owing to absentee landlords and the sending away of capital to the goldfields, little has been done in the direction of the application of science to the agriculture of the colony. Farming in Natal is thus described in the recently issued Report of the Industries and Tariff Revision Commission:—

> "Farming in Natal as properly understood in these days is at the very beginning of its career. If the land and climate combined are to have a fair chance of yielding the latent wealth with which Nature has endowed this fertile Colony, then the primitive methods of the past must be abandoned, and new ones must be adopted on approved lines."

Evidence was brought before this Commission of the enormous carrying capacity of the land if only treated on proper principles. But the most isolated Indian raiat is not more conservative and hard to move than a certain class of Colonial farmer. All over South Africa is found this lack of science, these rough ways. They spoil Colonial fruit, they handicap Colonial wool, they make it easier for the butcher to deal with imported meat. Yet slowly these old methods will be abandoned. There are already signs of an awakening. The natives, too, cannot for ever exist in the way they do to-day. The pressure of population will drive them off the land or force them to adopt different ways of cultivation to make the land produce more. But will the rapid growth of the British Indian population help this movement ? At the outset it may. Yet as time goes on the pressure of the Indians must be felt more and more. If they do not drive out the white men already in Natal, they will at least undertake so much of the work of the colony that no fresh European blood will be needed. As an outlet for England's surplus population Natal will be useless.

And again must be emphasized the point that the spreading of the Indian over South Africa has been accomplished in the face of strong local prejudice and specially devised legislative enactments. What if these barriers are removed or made less formidable ?

There is one other point—the danger to the Empire by the lessening of the value of a colony to the English manufacturer. The West Indies have proved that the indentured Asiatic can increase the purchasing capacity of a tropical country. But the white man remains the biggest buyer.

In the end the colony with the largest Asiatic population where white men should dwell will be of least value to the Empire. It is an economic axiom that the white man consumes more than the

Asiatic. The trade of a colony with a big white population must be more remunerative to England than that of a colony where a decreasing white population is struggling hard against the competition of the Eastern peoples. The following table shows the approximate returns of contributions to public revenue in relation to the internal trade of Natal, and in combination with the oversea and overberg trade, for a period of ten years :—

PER HEAD OF POPULATION.

	Europeans or Whites (including "mixed or other")			Indians and Asiatics.		
	£	s.	d.	£	s.	d.
1895 . . .	19	8	4	1	1	2
1896 . . .	23	5	6	1	3	1
1897 . . .	34	13	4	1	0	3
1898 . . .	27	2	11	1	2	8
1899 . . .	27	6	3	1	3	3
1900 . . .	21	11	0	1	5	7
1901 . . .	32	0	11	1	10	4
1902 . . .	33	17	9	1	14	2
1903 . . .	40	6	3	1	10	8
1904 . . .	34	10	7	1	5	11

	£	s.	d.
Average per head for ten years—Europeans, etc.	30	11	4
,, ,, ,, ,, Asiatics . .	1	6	4½
The native average for the same period was .	0	9	6¾

An Indianized Natal or an Australia overrun by Chinese or Japanese would be of less value commercially to Great Britain than if the lands were inhabited by white races. And added to this must come the question of defence. In the rebellion of the natives in Natal this year it was pointed out that the adult male natives in the colony exceeded the adult whites by 150,000. The putting down of the outbreak threw a severe strain on the military and police forces of the country. Will the situation not be more difficult the greater is the Indian population, with its corollary the lessened openings for white men who could form part of the militia ? Or must Asiatics be admitted to the privilege of taking a share in the defences of the colony ?

Looked at from all standpoints, with special regard to the future, the presence of a large Asiatic population in those colonies which can be considered as White Man's Country is a distinct danger to the colony concerned and to the welfare of the Empire itself. The attitude of Sir Henry Parkes is the safest :—

> " . . . It is our duty to preserve the type of the British nation, and we ought not for any consideration whatever to admit any element that would detract from, or in any appreciable degree lower, that admirable type of nationality.
>
> " We should not encourage or admit amongst us any class of persons whatever whom we are not prepared to advance to all our franchises, to all our privileges as citizens, and all our social rights, including the right of marriage. I maintain that no class of persons should be

admitted here, so far as we can reasonably exclude them, who cannot come amongst us, take up all our rights, perform on a ground of equality all our duties, and share in our august and lofty work of founding a free nation.

"We cannot patiently stand to be treated with the frozen indifference of persons who consider some petty quarrel in a petty state of more importance than the gigantic interests of these magnificent Colonies."

CHAPTER VIII

WHAT IS THE REMEDY ?

> "The reference made to . . . international engagements induces me to observe that the exceptional legislation that has been adopted by the majority of the Australasian Colonies on the subject of Chinese immigration does not violate any recognized rule of international comity; on the contrary, it is a fundamental maxim of International Law that 'every State has the right to regulate immigration to its territories as is most convenient to the safety and prosperity of the country, without regard to the Municipal Law of the country whence the immigration proceeds'" (*see* Ferguson's *Manual of International Law*, vol. i. p. 130, and Calvo's *Droit Intern.*, vol. l. liv. viii.).—Attorney-General of Tasmania, 1888.

THE danger of Asiatic immigration on a large scale is the most important problem which affects the Colonies as a whole. The present generation has the power of influencing the conditions under which the next must live. But on question of defence, on tariffs, on taxation and other matters the error of to-day can be neutralized by the legislation of to-morrow. Yet once throw the door open to the East, once admit Asiatics in the mass, and a country has accepted a burden which must ever grow heavier. Under the Natal system it is difficult to prevent the ousting of the white artisan. In 1896 the Tongaat Sugar Company in Natal applied to the Immigration Trust Board for the following Indian artisans :—

Bricklayer,
Platelayer,
Plasterer,
House painter,
Carriage builder,
Wheelwright,
Carpenter,
Blacksmith,
Fitter,
Turner,
Iron moulder,
Coppersmith.

The application was granted, but the indignation aroused in the colony was so great that it was withdrawn by the Sugar Company. And even if the contract coolie is confined to unskilled labour, the free Indian is under no restrictions, and his competition reduces the number of openings available for white men. "The vegetables, fruits and fish that adorn a Natal dinner table are grown, caught and hawked by coolies; the table linen is washed by another coolie; and in all probability the guests would be served by coolie waiters and partake of fare provided by a coolie cook." [1] It is sometimes argued that the white man ought not to have to do the rough work, that his proper position is that of

[1] *D. F. News*, January, 1897.

overseer or idler. In a speech made at Stanger in Natal, in 1897, a Mr. Clayton [1] said :—

> "He was pretty confident that his children, rather than have to work any land he might be able to leave them, would prefer to let it to Indians at reasonable rents."

If this is the principle to be generally accepted, it would be well to at once cease all efforts to attract European immigrants to South Africa, for there are quite sufficient whites there now to do all the supervising necessary. But if Canada had imported cheap Asiatic labour to do the rough work on the land, would it be a country with the grand prospects it has to-day? If Australasia had freely admitted the Chinese and the Japanese, would it be of any value at all to the surplus population of Great Britain—would it even be able to provide work for the people it has? Difficult the question undoubtedly is, especially when the people against whom barriers are erected are British subjects. "The problem," wrote the Johannesburg *Star* nine years ago when dealing with the Natal agitation, "which presents itself to Mr. Chamberlain is therefore by no means easy of solution. Morally, Mr. Chamberlain is bound to uphold the righteousness of the Indians' position; economically, he is forced to admit the justice of the Colonists' claim; politically, it passes the wit of man to decide which side to favour."

[1] Memorial to Mr. Joseph Chamberlain from the British-Indians in Natal *re* Anti-Indian Demonstration.

The need for some solution of the problem is greater to-day than it was at the time of the Natal agitation in 1896, when the colony had only 50,000 Indians compared with the 100,000 to-day. The back door has been open so long that Natal's Indian population has become the biggest obstacle to South African Federation; indeed, judging by the feeling in the inland colonies it will be an insuperable barrier. On the other hand, it is unfair to overlook the good which Indian competition and Indian labour has done. The Natal Commissioners who reported on Indian trading twenty years ago pointed out how their "tact and energy" had reduced the price of rice from 21*s*. per bag to 14*s*., and remarked: "It is said that Kaffirs can buy from Arabs at from 25 to 30 per cent. lower rates than those obtaining six or seven years ago." The Commissioners added: "We are content to place on record our strong opinion, based on much observation, that the presence of these traders has been beneficial to the whole Colony, and that it would be unwise, if not unjust, to legislate to their prejudice."

Yet it must be remembered that testimonials of this character related to a period when Asiatic competition was less marked than it is to-day. Conditions have changed since then. There has arisen that ideal of Colonial Nationalism which can never be realized if the white population is restricted by the presence of a mass of Asiatics. Admitting all the good work done by the Indians in Natal in the past does not logically bind one to support further immigration on the same scale.

Granted that the existing Asiatic population is hard-working, thrifty and law-abiding, one may still believe that a further influx would be harmful.

What, then, are the restrictions needed? Up to last year the restrictions in the different White Man's Colonies of the Empire were based on the same principles. The prohibitive clauses are these:—

AUSTRALIA.

Immigration Restriction Act, 1901, Clause 3 (*a*).—"Any person who when asked to do so by an officer fails to write out at dictation and sign in the presence of the officer a passage of fifty words in length in a European language directed by the officer."

NEW ZEALAND.

Clause 3 (1).—"Any person other than of British (including Irish) birth and parentage who when asked to do so by an officer appointed under this Act by the Governor fails to himself write out and sign in the presence of such officer in any European language an application in the form numbered two in the schedule hereto or in such other form as the Colonial Secretary from time to time directs:

"Provided that any person dissatisfied with the decision of such officer shall have the right to appeal to the nearest stipendiary magistrate who shall make such inquiries as he shall think fit, and his decision thereon shall be final."

H

Cape Colony.

Immigration Act, Clause 2 (*a*).—"Any person who when asked to do so by a duly authorized officer shall be unable through deficient education to himself write out and sign in the characters of a European language an application to the satisfaction of the Minister."

Natal.

Immigration Restriction Act of 1903, Clause 5 (*a*).—" Any person who when asked to do so by any duly authorized officer shall be unable to himself write out and sign in the characters of some European language an application to the satisfaction of the Minister."

These clauses have proved effective, with one exception. The system of indentured labour prevailing in Natal means that the back door of South Africa is left wide open. Asiatics pour in as indentured coolies and at the end of five years become free men. With the Chinese labourers on the Rand there is not this leakage. The indentures terminate in China, and not a man is entitled to remain in the colony, or to compete with white men. The Chinese are brought in under special conditions to meet an exceptional difficulty. They are well housed and fed, and they can earn anything between 30*s*. and several pounds a month—one hammer boy makes about £120 a year, but he is an abnormal worker—whereas at the Raub mine in Pahang the Chinese underground men receive only 1*s*. a day and the surface hand 10*d.* and have to find their own food and housing, whilst at Rawang in Selangor the Chinese tin workers receive 1*s.* 1*d.* a day and find their own food and supplies. Nothing shows more clearly the ignorance of South African opinion which prevails at Home than the suggestion that the Chinese should only be allowed to work the mines under contracts similar to those prevailing in the West Indies. The British Guiana contracts, as has already been seen, are more likely to induce permanent settlement than even those in Natal. The free labourer idea would mean that in an astonishingly short space of time the Transvaal would have 100,000 to 150,000 Chinese. It might be an admirable thing for the mine shareholders; but it would be inflicting a punishment on the white people of the colony which nothing could justify. It is difficult to see upon what line of reasoning, or principle of justice or policy, it is thought necessary that the Chinese coolies should be free to settle down in the Transvaal and undertake any kind of work. The essentials are just and kind treatment, fair conditions of labour, and the prevention of those outrages which at first marred the experiment. The coolies to-day have the opportunity of earning more money than they could in any other part of the world, and at the end of their term could if they chose take home a sum which would make them men of importance in their own districts. Why for the sake of a gratuitous sentimentalism insist upon conditions which can bring only incalculable injury upon the whole of South Africa?

There are two important considerations in dealing with the Asiatic question in the Colonies. The first is to prevent a further influx into those lands which may be fairly regarded as White Man's Country. In the West Indies the difficulty is not the same. The Asiatics have increased the prosperity of a land which cannot absorb a surplus white population—whether time will show that even here a mistake was made one cannot prophesy. But in South Africa, Australia, Canada, and British Columbia the door must be gently and firmly closed against a horde of Asiatics who must always remain a community apart. This can be done by insisting that the indentures of contract labourers shall terminate in the country from which they came. There is nothing harsh or unjust in this. It is simply a business proposition in the real interests of the country. The labour supply in South Africa, inadequate as it is to-day, will in time, by the natural increase of the large native population and the gradual training of the Bantu to more regular work, become sufficient. The 50,000 or 60,000 Chinese who now keep the Rand mines going are not wanted for all time; the Indian labour which swarms over Natal may be useful to this generation, but it will sadly trouble a future. The attitude of the Indian Government is not set sternly against a system by which indentures terminate in India. When the Transvaal opened negotiations for 10,000 coolies from India to work on the railways "under an indenture providing for their repatriation on the termination of their period of service" the objection was not to the proposed form of contract. The words of Mr. Lyttelton's despatch are : " . . . The Government of India was not prepared to meet the wishes of the Transvaal Government *while the position of British-Indian traders resident in the Transvaal remained in so unsatisfactory a state*" (Cd. 2239). The Government of India asks for the following conditions for the Indians in the Transvaal :—

> 1. "The abolition of registration for Indians generally, and the substitution therefor of a measure for keeping undesirable persons out of the Colony.
>
> 2. "Securing that locations for Asiatics should be restricted to those classes for whom they are required on sanitary grounds.
>
> 3. "Allowing business to be carried on outside locations.
>
> 4. "Replacing the restrictions on the acquisition of real property by Asiatics by a general law against speculative acquisition.
>
> 5. "Exempting better-class Asiatics from all special restrictions and allowing them to have Indian servants to reside with them."

These conditions would not perhaps meet with the approval of the Transvaal, but probably the Indian Government could be induced to accept slight modifications, especially regarding the servant question, which would be open to abuse, as the Chinese abused the regulations in Australia, and all Asiatics break those which exist to-day in

Portuguese East Africa. But somewhat upon these lines a reasonable solution could be arrived at, providing first for the exclusion (or if admitted as indentured labourers, the repatriation) of future masses of Asiatics; secondly, giving easier conditions to the Asiatics already in the Colonies, especially the better-class population. The rulers of South Africa have favoured some such solution. Lord Milner wrote in May, 1904:—

> "I thought it would be possible, by giving to Asiatics of a superior class a special status, and treating them virtually like Europeans, to avoid, at any rate, the appearance of race legislation. I still believe that, if the European, and especially the British, population in this country could be induced to see the matter in a reasonable light, such a course would provide not indeed a perfect, but a fairly satisfactory, solution of the difficulty. It is not, in my opinion, an influx of Asiatics of the upper and middle classes (professional men and merchants, as distinct from small traders) which really threaten this community. If by treating this class liberally we could induce the Government of India to acquiesce in the virtual exclusion of the petty trader class, who are out of place here, and at the same time to agree to the introduction, under conditions ensuring their ultimate return to their native country, of Indian labourers whom we greatly need, and who could earn in this country such wages as they can

obtain nowhere else in the world, I believe that the arrangement would be beneficial both to the Transvaal and to India.

"This view is consistent with the opinions I hold on the colour question generally. I think that to attempt to place coloured people on an equality with white in South Africa is wholly impracticable, and that, moreover, it is in principle wrong. But I also hold that when a coloured man possesses a certain high grade of civilization he ought to obtain what I call 'white privileges,' irrespective of his colour. I have on more than one occasion given expression to these views. They are very unpopular in the Transvaal at the present time, but I do not despair of their ultimately prevailing."

Sir Arthur Lawley was, in the Transvaal, regarded as "safer" than the late High Commissioner on the Asiatic question, but his view ran much on the same lines :—

> "Speaking generally" (he said) "I am convinced that a *modus vivendi* is only possible by a compromise, and that the basis of a compromise which will be acceptable to the Europeans of the Transvaal must be to treat fairly those Indians who have been allowed to come into the country, and to let any future immigrants know the disabilities under which they will be allowed to enter the Transvaal."

Lord Selborne, speaking at Krugersdorp in October, 1905, said :—

> "As regarded the Indians already in the country before the war the British Government over and over again pressed on the Government of the South African Republic measures for the amelioration of the condition of the British-Indians already in the country, and asserted its duty to protect them. They might approve or disapprove of that action of Her late Majesty's Government. So far as he was aware it was undoubtedly approved by the general body of the British public opinion in South Africa. Now, he asked them, as fair men, would it be consistent with honour if now that the country belonged to the British Empire the Government, and himself as representing the King, were to turn round and deal with the British-Indians in the country differently to the manner in which they always pressed President Kruger to deal with them?"

Lord Selborne admitted: "It is a matter of distress to me, of sorrow to me, that in any respect the splendid theory of absolute equality between all British subjects should in practice have to be departed from." But he also said:—

> "It is to the interests not only of South Africa, not only of the British Empire as a whole, it is to the interest of India as one of the most important parts of the Empire, that this subject should be dealt with, not by force or on theory, but with the recognition of the facts, and carrying public opinion in the Trans-

> vaal behind it, because after all, true as it is that the British Indian has a right as a British subject, it is also equally true that the Transvaaler has a right as a British subject, and any consideration of this question that only took in the British-Indian point of view would be of no avail if the greatest weight were not also given to the opinion of that British in whose own country the particular controversy has arisen."

There would no doubt be objections raised in India to the recruiting of labour on indentures which provided for repatriation on the termination of the contract; there may be protests, perhaps, in the future, from India, China, and Japan at Exclusion Acts. There will also be opposition in South Africa to the least relaxation of the somewhat harsh laws aimed at Asiatics. The General Dealers Bill in the Cape gives the Indian or Chinese trader very little liberty in his business, and the location proposals in the Transvaal would inevitably end in loss for which adequate compensation could not be obtained. But the essential thing is for the Imperial Government to support the Colonies in the ideal of a White Man's Country. South Africa can never be that in the sense in which Australasia and Canada are, for the native problem is always present. But it can at least be kept as white as possible, and the native question can be complicated as little as possible by the presence of thousands of Asiatics.

What is needed to-day is the sympathy and

assistance of the Home Government in maintaining the united, settled policy of all the great colonies of the Empire. The tropical colonies—the Plantations—may decide their own course. But do not impose upon those lands which aim to be a White Man's Country conditions which would make their ideal but an idle dream. Three principles should be borne in mind :—

1. Keep out masses of Asiatics as permanent residents as far as possible at all costs.

2. If indentured labour is needed, insist upon repatriation on expiration of contract.

3. Fair, even generous, treatment to those Asiatics who have under the conditions of the old days become part of the population of the country.

This is a policy which can be understood. It is based on the principle of self-preservation, not on prejudice to colour, or religion, or habits of life. This is the stand for the Colonies to make. Admit that the Asiatic has in many parts worked well for us, in some parts is still welcome to-day. But, setting aside colour prejudice or narrow-minded bigotry of race, the Colonies capable of supporting a white British population must declare that, on the highest ground, the future of the country and their Empire, they cannot open wide the door to inferior masses who, with all their virtues, will underlive and undersell them. With such a policy there must be no vexatious restrictions to insult the educated man—things more irritating and harmful than the regulation which quietly keeps out thousands of the poorer class. The cultured traveller of the Eastern world ought not to have to submit to treatment which is not even meted out to a pauper immigrant on a New York quay. He should not have to consent to having his thumb impressions taken like a criminal, or be threatened, as the extremists of the Transvaal threaten him, with instant removal to a location, no matter whether he be a judge of the Indian Bench or the prince of the Rajput family considered sufficiently civilized to entertain the future King and Queen of England.

An influx of Asiatics inevitably means first a lowering of the standard of living for the white worker, and then his gradual elimination; it means that the country becomes of no value to the Empire as a home for the surplus population of the United Kingdom; and in the end it means that it becomes a diminished commercial asset, and a greater strain upon the defensive forces of England.

The Asiatic immigrant in the West Indies or Malaya or Borneo may be of more value than the native; but the Asiatic immigrant in Australasia or South Africa or Canada can never be as valuable to the Empire as the white man. To encourage the Asiatic at the expense of the Englishman is a policy which can only end in the loss of the Colonial Empire.

APPENDIX I

BRITISH-INDIAN CLAIMS AND COMPLAINTS

THE following is the full text of the Statement and Addendum submitted by the British-Indian Deputation to the Transvaal Constitution Committee:—

1. The British Indian Association has always admitted the principle of white predominance and has therefore no desire to press, on behalf of the community it represents, for any political rights for the sake of them. But past experience shows that in a colony enjoying self-government, communities that have no voice in the choice of representatives have been very largely neglected.

2. There is in the Transvaal at the present moment an estimated population of over 12,000 British-Indians. Before war, the adult Indian population was 15,000.

3. The first Indian settlers found their way into the Transvaal in the early eighties.

4. They were then free from restrictions of any kind whatsoever.

5. But by their successful enterprise, they aroused the jealousy of white traders, and soon there sprang up an anti-Indian agitation, initiated by Chambers of Commerce wherein the British element was predominant.

6. As result, the Government of the late President Kruger approached Her late Majesty's Government for permission to pass legislation restrictive of the liberty of British-Indians. They proposed to interpret the term "Natives," occurring in the London Convention to include Asiatics.

7. This contention Her Majesty's advisers rejected, but they were not unwilling for " sanitary reasons " to sanction legislation restricting Asiatics as to their residence to bazaars or location with the proviso that British-Indians of the trader class should be left entirely free.

8. As a result of these negotiations Law 3 of 1885 as amended in 1886 was passed.

9. Immediately it became known, a strong protest went up from British-Indians.

10. It was then realized that the Law was, contrary to the expectations of Her late Majesty's Government, sought to be enforced against all British-Indians.

11. Then followed a series of strong representations by Her late Majesty's Government, addressed to the late Boer Government, culminating in the matter being submitted to the arbitration of the then Chief Justice of the Orange River Colony.

12. Between 1885 and 1895, therefore, the Law 3 of 1885 practically remained a dead letter although the Boer Government always threatened to enforce it.

13. The award of the arbitrator did not define the legal position. But it left the question of interpretation of Law 3 of 1885 to the Courts of the late Republic.

14. British-Indians again appealed to the British Government for protection.

15. Mr. Chamberlain, whilst he declined to disturb the ward, did not abandon the case for the Indian subjects of Her late Majesty. In his despatch dated September 4, 1895, he stated :—

" In conclusion, I would say, that whilst desirous loyally to abide by the award, and to allow it to close the legal and international question in dispute between the two Governments, I reserve to myself the liberty later on to make friendly representations to the South African Republic as to the traders, and possibly to invite the Government to consider whether, when once its legal position has been made good, it would not be wise to review the situation from a new point of view, and decide whether it would not be better in the interests of its own burghers to treat the Indians more generously, and to free itself from even the appearance of countenancing a trade jealousy which I have some reason to believe does not emanate from the governing class in the Republic."

This was in 1895.

16. Owing then to such representations, which continued up to the time of the war, the Law in question was never effectively enforced, and Indians traded and lived where they liked, in spite of the prohibition contemplated by it.

17. But an enforcement of the Law being imminent in 1899, it was, among other things, a subject for discussion at the Bloemfontein Conference, which preceded the war. The subject was considered so important by Lord Milner, that when the question of franchise to the Uitlanders seemed to admit of a settlement, Lord Milner cabled that the question of the status of coloured British subjects was still outstanding.

18. Lord Lansdowne declared that it was a contributory cause of war.

19. At the close of the war, and at the time of the Vereeniging compact, His Majesty's Government informed the Boer representatives that the status of coloured persons should be the same in the two colonies as at the Cape.

20. But to-day the position is worse than before war.

21. The Progressive party, from which at least Indians, as fellow-loyalists and fellow-sufferers before war, may claim a fair measure of justice, has stated it as an item of its programme that the liberty of British-Indians should be specifically restricted. If its desires were carried out, the position, bad as it is to-day, would be much worse then.

22. From the Dutch party it is now impossible to expect any measure of reasonableness.

23. Under Responsible Government, then, British-Indians and others similarly situated, unless they are specially protected, stand practically little chance of justice being done to them.

24. It would, therefore, seem that the granting of the

franchise to British-Indians would be the most natural means of protecting their interests.

25. It has been urged that the treaty of Vereeniging precludes the possibility of any such provision being made.

26. But it is respectfully submitted that the term "natives," whatever else it may mean, can never include British-Indians.

27. The statute-book of the colony is replete with laws which deal with the "natives," but which admittedly do not apply to Asiatics or British-Indians.

28. The fact that Law 3 of 1885 deals specially with Asiatics and does not apply to the "natives," shows, too, that the Transvaal laws have almost invariably distinguished between "natives" and "Asiatics."

29. Indeed, whereas natives can, owing to the meaning that the term has borne, hold landed property in the Transvaal, Asiatics cannot.

30. Thus, therefore, so far as the Vereeniging compact is concerned, there appears to be no justification whatever for depriving the Indians of the franchise.

31. But the Committee of the British-Indian Association is well aware of the almost unanimous hostility of white races against provision being made in the Constitution for a grant of the franchise to British-Indians.

32. If, therefore, such a grant be considered impossible, it is absolutely essential that, apart from the orthodox reservatory clause as to the power of veto over all *class* legislation, there should be a special clause which shall be a living reality, and which, instead of being exercised only on the rarest occasions, should ensure the fullest protection to the British-Indian settlers as to their right to own landed property, freedom of movement, and freedom of trade, subject to such safeguards of a *general* nature as may be considered necessary, and are made applicable to all, irrespective of race or colour.

33. Then, and only then, will it be possible, apart from the inherent right that every British subject should have to ordinary civil rights in British dominions, for His

Majesty's advisers to redeem the promises specifically made to British-Indians as to their status in the Transvaal.

34. Much of what has been stated above applies to the position of British-Indians in the Orange River Colony.

35. There the Indian has no rights, save as a domestic servant. An elaborate anti-Asiatic law deprives him of practically all civil liberty.

(Sd.) ABDUL GANIE, President B.I.A.
„ E. S. CCOVADIA.
„ H. C. ALLY.
„ EBRAHIM H. KHOTA.
„ E. M. PATEL.
„ E. M. JOSSEP.
„ J. A. PATEL.
„ M. K. GANDHI.

APPENDIX "A"

For authorities in support of the facts cited in the foregoing statement, the Deputation beg to refer the Constitution Committee to the following :—

1. Transvaal Green Book, No. 1 of 1894.
2. Transvaal Green Book, No. 2 of 1894.
3. Blue Book on Grievances of British-Indians in the Transvaal, published in 1896.
4. Blue Book containing Correspondence relating to British-Indians in the Transvaal.—Cd. 2239.
5. Laws and Volksraad Resolutions, etc., relating to "Natives and Coolies" (a separate Government publication).
6. Chapter XXXIII, p. 199, Laws of the Orange River Colony.

APPENDIX "B"

The following is a comparison of the position of British-Indians in the Transvaal under Boer and under British rule :—

Before the War.	Under British Rule.
(1) Indians were free to enter the country without restriction.	(1) No Immigration permitted other than of *bona fide* refugees who left on the eve of the war, and they are only admitted gradually and after long delay for the consideration of their applications. Permits are required even for little children, and every Indian has to attach his thumb impression on these documents.
(2) Payment of registration fee not enforced.	(2) Registration fee of £3, on pain of fine not exceeding £100, or imprisonment for not more than six months, strictly enforced. Attempt is being made now to exact registration fees from Indian women, and to require them to take out permits.
(3) Landed property could be held in the names of Europeans.	(3) The law against Asiatics holding real property strictly enforced, even in cases where land is required for religious purposes.
(4) Indians held 99 years' leases for landed property in location or bazaar in Johannesburg.	(4) These leases have been expropriated under the Insanitary Area Commissioners' Report, without the owners' receiving equal title elsewhere in Johannesburg in a suitable position.
(5) No separate inquisitorial Asiatic Department.	(5) Office of Registrar of Asiatics established; is arbitrary in procedure and delays the settlement of individual applications, permits, etc.
(6) Many harsh legislative restrictions allowed to remain	(6) Inoperative Boer enactments brought into force, and

inoperative owing largely to British intervention.	rendered more stringent by Ordinances or Executive Orders, and British Indians offensively classed in legislation with Kaffirs, savages, and semi-civilized races.

ADDENDUM

The following addendum was prepared at the instance of the Constitution Committee :—

1. The Commissioners seem to be under the impression that British-Indians have full rights in the Transvaal.

2. Unfortunately, as will appear from the schedule attached to the statement, British-Indians have very few civil rights—we venture to recapitulate the civil disabilities :—

3. (1) British-Indians cannot own landed property, including even long leases, except in locations or streets set apart for them.

(2) There are no streets set apart, but there are locations far away from town, like the Continental Ghettos. And in these, too, except in one or two places, Indians are only monthly squatters. In Pretoria and Potchefstroom alone do they receive twenty-one years' leases. In Germiston, they have even received notices not to receive any tenants on their stands. The notice reads as follows :—

> "You are hereby notified that you are not permitted to sublet rooms to natives or others. Such sub-letting to any person is a breach of the contract under which you are allowed to hold a stand, and renders you liable to have your stand permit cancelled, and yourself expelled from this location."

(3) So much is this prohibition carried out in practice, that Indians are unable to have their mosques transferred in the names of Indian trustees.

(4) Indians have to pay a registration fee of £3 on arrival in this country. The Government has now threat-

ened even to require women and children to take out registration certificates.

(5) Indians in Pretoria and Johannesburg are prohibited by law from walking on the footpaths. They, however, do make use of them on sufferance. An attempt was only recently made to prevent them from using the footpaths.

(6) Indians are not allowed to make use of the tram cars in Pretoria.

(7) They are prevented in Johannesburg from riding on the ordinary cars, but special trailer cars are occasionally run for coloured people.

(8) It was contended on behalf of the Indians, that, under the ordinary bye-laws, they could insist on riding on the tram cars. The Town Council opposed the contention on the ground that certain smallpox regulations that were promulgated by the late Dutch Government in 1897 were still in force. The matter was twice tested before the magistrate at Johannesburg, and each time the Town Council lost. It has therefore now met the Indians by cancelling the bye-laws regulating the traffic on the tram cars. In order to gain its end, the Town Council is now running the Municipal cars without any bye-laws whatsoever. Whether, under the common law, Indians will be able now to make good their right or not is an open question.

It is worthy of note that the above-mentioned cancelling bye-law was surreptitiously published in the following manner :—

"Prior to the 9th May, 1906, in accordance with Section 22 of Proclamation 16 of 1901, a notice had been published in a newspaper circulating in the Municipality setting forth the general purport of these proposed amendments and stating that they were open to inspection at the office of the Council."

On the 9th inst., a meeting of the Town Council was held. The notice was apparently advertised in such a manner as to render it almost a matter of impossibility for parties concerned to challenge the proposed amendments, owing chiefly to the fact that no report of them had appeared in the ordinary columns of the newspapers, and to the further fact that, as will be seen, the proposal came through the Works Committee, instead of the Tramways and Lighting Committee, which would ordinarily concern itself with Tramway Regulations as it has done in the past.

On the occasion of the aforesaid Council meeting, the Works Committee brought forward the proposed amendment, on the following pretext :—

> " Since the Tramway System was taken over by the Municipal Council, the Traffic Bye-laws applicable to tram cars are no longer required as they were only intended for application to private tram cars. It is proposed, therefore, that the Bye-laws should be amended accordingly."

The proposals were submitted at the end of a long agenda, when even the most vigilant councillor might have been lulled into a sense of security, especially in view of the seemingly innocuous nature of the preamble, and passed without comment. A notice appeared in the Government *Gazette* of the 18th inst. adopting the proposed cancelling bye-law, and giving it the force of law. The whole matter, therefore, was settled practically behind the backs of the British-Indians within a period of nine days, for all practical purposes, without warning.

(9) Attempt is now being made to expropriate what is known as the Malay Location in Johannesburg, which has a large Indian population, and to send the Indians to a place thirteen miles away from Johannesburg.

(10) Whereas formerly Indians were free to immigrate into the Transvaal, at present the Peace Preservation Ordinance, which is purely a political law, is being wrested from its legitimate purpose to prevent Indians from entering the Transvaal. Not only are new Indians being prevented from entering the country, but the following exceptional hardships are imposed on all residents of the Transvaal :—

(*a*) There are no published regulations regarding the administration of the ordinance.

(*b*) It changes according to the whims or prejudices of the officials administering it.

The following is, therefore, the practice in vogue to-day:

(I) Indians who were in the Transvaal before war and who paid £3 for registration, are prevented from returning unless they can prove absolutely that they left on the outbreak of hostilities.

(II) Those who are allowed to enter the Transvaal have to put their thumb impressions upon their applications, as also upon their permits, and they are required to put them each time they enter the Transvaal. This is applicable to all Indians without regard to their position and without regard to the fact whether they can sign their names in English or not. An England-returned Indian gentleman who spoke English well, and who is a very well known merchant, was twice obliged to put his thumb impression.

(III) Wives and children under twelve years of such Indians are now required to take out separate permits.

(IV) Children, twelve years old or over, of such Indians are not allowed to join or accompany their parents.

(V) Indian merchants are not allowed to import any trustworthy clerks or managers unless the latter are themselves such as fall within the first clause hereinbefore referred to.

(VI) Even those who are allowed to enter have to wait for months before they are permitted to enter the country.

(VII) Even temporary permits are refused to Indians of respectability. Mr. Suliman Manga, who is studying for the Bar in London, wishing to pass through the Transvaal on his way to Delagoa Bay, was refused a permit when his case was considered as of a British subject. When it became known that he was a Portuguese subject, for fear, evidently, of international complications, he was granted a temporary permit.

(VIII) Such is the terrible position of British-Indians who are resident in the Transvaal. It is growing daily worse, and unless the Imperial Government is willing and ready to protect them, the ultimate result can only be slow extinction.

(11) The following facts will show what the Europeans of the Transvaal will do, if they are left to themselves :—

The National Convention, which specially met to consider the Asiatic question, passed the following resolutions :—

> (1st) "That having regard to the preponderance of the native races in this country, the difficulties surrounding the settlement of native policy, the necessity for protecting the existing European population and encouraging further European immigration, this Convention affirms the principle that Asiatic immigration should be prohibited except under the provisions of the Labour Importation Ordinance.
>
> (2nd) "That this Convention having regard to the importance of arriving at a permanent and conclusive settlement of the whole question and of preventing any further attempts to reopen the matter, recommends that the Government be invited to take into consideration the advisability of removing into bazaars all Asiatic traders, compensation being provided for such as may have vested interests which have been legally acquired prior to the war.
>
> (3rd) "That this Convention, recognizing the grave danger resulting from the continued issue of trading licences to Asiatics permitting trade outside bazaars, requests the Government to take immediate steps to pass the necessary legal enactments to prevent any further issue of such licences and that with regard to the appointment of any proposed Commission to deal with the Asiatic question, this Convention urges upon the Government the necessity for including therein men, other than officials, with a thorough knowledge of existing conditions in South Africa.
>
> (4th) "That this Convention affirms its opinion that all Asiatics should be required to reside in bazaars."

(*a*) The following is the declared policy of the Progressive Party :—

The restriction of immigration of Asiatics into the Transvaal, except in the case of indentured labourers who are subject to repatriation at the expiration of their contract, and the regulation of Asiatic trading licences.

(*b*) The people of Potchefstroom once met together, created a disturbance, and even broke the windows of Indian stores.

(*c*) The Europeans of Boksburg wish to remove Indians from their present location, which they occupied before war, to a site far away from town where trade is utterly impossible, and they have more than once threatened to use physical force should an Indian attempt to open a store outside the location.

(12) In the main statement, the Deputation has urged that past experience shows that the deprivation of the franchise and the orthodox power of veto have been totally inadequate to protect Indians.

(13) We will venture now to give instances :—

In Natal, after the grant of Responsible Government, Indians were virtually deprived of the franchise. The late Sir John Robinson, in supporting the Bill, said that by disfranchising Indians, every member of the Natal Parliament became a trustee for Indians.

Soon after the Bill became an Act of Parliament, the trust was thus discharged :—

(*a*) An annual poll-tax of £3 was imposed on all indentured Indians who entered after its promulgation, to be payable on the termination of their indentures, unless they returned to India or re-indentured themselves.

(*b*) An Immigration Restriction Act was passed prohibiting all who did not possess a knowledge of one of the European languages from entering Natal unless they were formerly domiciled in the colony.

(*c*) A Dealers' Licences Act was passed which gave absolute powers to the Town Councils or Licensing Boards to control trade licences. It ousts the jurisdiction of the

Supreme Court. Ostensibly applying to all traders, it is enforced only against Indians. And under it, no Indian, however well established, is ever secure as to his licence from year's end to year's end.

Against all this legislation, the Imperial Government has felt powerless to protect British-Indians.

(14) Whether Indians are granted the franchise under the Constitution or not, a special clause protecting vested interests is absolutely necessary.

(15) No colony on the eve of receiving self-government has presented the features that the Transvaal and Orange River Colonies present.

(16) All the causes for which the war took place have not been removed. Anti-Indian legislation of the Transvaal was one of the causes.

(17) Promise made by the Home Government that Indians and other coloured people in the two colonies should be treated the same way as those at the Cape, has not yet been redeemed.

(18) Negotiations were actually pending between the Home Government and the Local Governments as to the removal of the disabilities of British-Indians when His Majesty's new Ministers decided to grant Responsible Government to the two colonies, and the negotiations have therefore been suspended or dropped altogether.

(19) The position at the Cape is that Indians have equal rights with the Europeans, i.e. :—

(*a*) They have the same franchise rights as the Europeans.

(*b*) They are under the same Immigration Restriction Act as the Europeans.

(*c*) They have equal rights with the latter to hold landed property and to trade.

(*d*) They have full freedom of locomotion from place to place.

Dated at Johannesburg this 29th day of May, 1906.

APPENDIX II

ARGUMENTS FOR AND AGAINST ASIATIC COMPETITION

AGAINST

THE following article appeared in the *Rand Daily Mail* (Johannesburg) in July, 1906:—

"There has of late been some controversy regarding the real extent of Asiatic competition in South Africa. Denial follows assertion with monotonous regularity, but the impartial investigator meets with little in the nature of irrefutable evidence. On the one hand we hear of the enormous growth of Asiatic trading and the closing down of European businesses to an ominous—though indefinite—extent. On the other we find the representatives of the British-Indian community declaring that the case has been exaggerated, and that in reality the presence of the Asiatic is beneficial to the country. Into the larger question of whether the advantage of cheaper labour in Natal more than compensates for the disadvantages of Indian trading we cannot for the moment enter. But in view of the certainty that the Transvaal as a self-governing colony will attempt to deal with the trading question—how far it will be allowed a free hand in the matter remains to be seen—it is interesting to see what is the precise evidence at the present time. It must be admitted that many of the figures which have been published are inaccurate. Some of the statistics given to the National Convention, and repeated again and again in meetings at Potchefstroom, Krugersdorp, and other towns, have been proved to be incorrect—a fact which, however, does not seem to prevent their still being quoted with the utmost complacency and confidence. When the Census reports for the whole of the colonies are issued the data available will be more complete. Yet even here the totals must be handled with some degree of caution, for the actual volume of trade done is not necessarily in the same ratio as the number of licences held.

"However, take the evidence as it stands. The Natal Census shows that there are in that colony 658 European general storekeepers, and 1,260 Asiatics similarly engaged. Many of the latter no doubt trade on so small a scale that no white man could live upon the profits secured. But the aggregate volume of business done by these 1,260 traders must be very considerable. Nor must it be forgotten that the competition would be still more overwhelming but for the Act passed in 1897, at the instance of Mr. Harry Escombe, giving an official of a municipality power to refuse to grant a licence—and from his decision there is no appeal. In theory, of course, the Act applies equally to Europeans and Asiatics. There is no outward evidence of class legislation; and at the time the British-Indian community probably did not realize its full meaning. For in practice no European is denied a licence, whereas the autocratic power given to the Municipality—power which lies with a white Town Council—often presses harshly on the Asiatic. The measure may or may not have been justified by expediency, but the point to remember is that in attempting to gauge the real operation of Asiatic competition allowance must be made for the restraining influence of this law. It may be argued that it is only fair to allow Indian traders to serve the Indian population which has built up the prosperity of the tea and sugar estates. But it is certain that the 1,260 general dealers cater for more than the Indian community, and it is impossible to avoid the conclusion that a large volume of trade which was formerly in the hands of the white population has passed into their hands.

"Turn to the Cape Colony. Amongst the causes of

depression in South Africa the over-trading of the past few years has been probably the greatest. In 1898 the Cape had 8,714 general dealers, importers, and agents. In 1905 there were 14,649. There was an increase of 68·1 per cent. in these vocations, whereas the imports retained in the colony for consumption only increased 25 per cent. in the same period. In these figures lies the secret of the depression. To blame the Asiatic for all this over-trading would be absurd. But the position of the non-European traders there throws some light on the larger problem. Figures were quoted in the Cape Parliament last week relating to the five largest trading centres in the colony—Capetown, East London, Kingwilliamstown, Kimberley, and Port Elizabeth. Last year in these towns 5,222 general dealers' licences were issued to Europeans. On May 1 this year the number had decreased to 3,920. In these five towns no fewer than 1,302 white men had gone out of business in a year. Now, in 1905 the licences issued to non-Europeans totalled 1,012, and on May 1 the aggregate was 1,059. Thus, whilst 1,302 Europeans had been forced to give up their licences, non-European traders thrived to such an extent that forty-four more entered the ranks of the general dealers. The reply may be that it was the failure of the Europeans which made suitable openings for the Asiatics. This may be so ; but it does not destroy the argument that the growth of Asiatic trading had in the first place something to do with the falling out of the white men. It was stated at a recent meeting of the Worcester Chamber of Commerce that one Indian in Capetown controlled twenty-nine shops. The Indian and Malay population alone cannot support the thousand odd Indian stores in the five towns, and undoubtedly a large share of the business done is with the white population. In the Transvaal the figures often quoted for Potchefstroom and other towns are wrong. But it is admitted that there are thirty-five Indian storekeepers in Pietersburg, and nineteen in Potchefstroom, and it would be idle to deny that this competition has driven out white traders. Johannesburg possesses 270 general dealers' businesses owned by Indians, and 255 owned by Chinese. The volume of business done cannot be estimated with any degree of accuracy. In the days of the Republic a petition presented to the Marquis of Ripon by British Indians stated that there were 200 traders whose liquidated assets would amount to nearly £100,000 ; and since that time Asiatic trading has vastly increased. We do not agree with those who charge the Indian or Asiatic storekeepers with filthy habits. Eleven years ago a petition signed by European firms in the Transvaal declared that the Indian traders 'keep their business places, as well as their residences, in a clean and proper sanitary state—in fact, just as good as the Europeans.' After all, dirt is not a monopoly of any race, and the ordinary powers of the sanitary authorities should be sufficient to deal with any cases of bad sanitation, whether the offenders belong to the Eastern or the Western peoples. Nor do we think the allegations of dishonest dealing can be sustained. Within a year it has been publicly complained in Pretoria and Durban that European wholesale houses give credit to Asiatics whilst refusing it to Europeans. One can hardly believe that wholesale houses prefer to be cheated by Indians than to trust honest Europeans.

"In considering the problem of Asiatic trading one must get rid of these prejudices and face the question from the standpoint of what is best for the country as a whole. It is impossible to prove that Asiatic competition does not press heavily on the European storekeepers in many parts of South Africa ; it is equally impossible to avoid the conclusion that but for the checks which are now enforced—against which the Indian community protests with a good deal of justice—that competition would be far more severe. The claim of the white population is that these restrictions are not sufficiently drastic ; the retort of the British-Indian community is to quote the pledges given by English statesmen before the war—pledges which committed the country to a line of action which was certainly not based upon local feeling. One must endeavour to remove gross injustice ;

but would the Home government be justified in refusing to permit any legislation demanded by the entire white population because of the statements made by the politicians of a former generation? If we are to be bound absolutely by the past we must carry out to-day the spirit of Sir G. Napier's Natal Proclamation of 1842: 'That there shall not be, in the eyes of the law, any distinction whatever founded on mere distinction of colour, origin, language, or creed, but that the protection of the law in letter and substance shall be extended impartially to all.' Theories of policy have changed since then. The latter-day policy is summed up in the words of Sir Arthur Lawley's despatch: 'If the redemption of the pledges upon which Sir M. M. Bhownaggree depends both in letter and spirit means that in fifty or a hundred years this country will have fallen to the inheritance of Eastern instead of Western populations, then from the point of view of civilization they must be numbered among promises which it is a greater crime to keep than to break.' Lord Selborne plainly told the British-Indians that the opinion of the Transvaal must carry the greater weight. In the end the local view must govern legislative action, care being taken to ensure a due consideration of vested interests. It will be impossible to force upon the Transvaal a policy to which the bulk of the inhabitants are strongly opposed. The Asiatic community—whether British subjects or not—should recognize the growing demand for Home Rule in the Colonies, and not make demands which they know will never be willingly conceded. With a little more moderation on both sides an unfortunate dispute may be avoided.'

A REPLY

The case for the British-Indian is given in the following reply which appeared in *Indian Opinion*, Natal:—

" In another column, we publish an able and eminently fair article on this subject, appearing in the leading columns of the *Rand Daily Mail* of Monday last. The writer has obviously written with great moderation and restraint, and we could wish most sincerely that all who argued the case against the Indian did so in the same temperate and statesmanlike spirit. Several points arising out of this article merit more than passing comment, for the issues presented are so serious as to demand the close application and attention of all who are moved with a desire to do justice fearlessly, and to put forth all the practical Christianity that is in them. We have felt all along that the spirit moving the opponents of Indians in South Africa is one depending far more on bitter race-prejudice and colour-hatred than on reasons based upon a proper appreciation of the economic features of the situation. We are glad to find that the *Rand Daily Mail* once for all brushes aside the foolish exaggerations given currency to at that preposterous meeting held under Mr. Loveday's *ægis* in 1904, dubbing itself falsely a 'National' Convention. When 'National' comes to bear the meaning 'parochial' and 'pettifogging,' perhaps we may grant that the Convention was right in its choice of an epithet. So that, for the present, we are to take it that statistics as presented and facts as set forth by the Convention are not to be taken seriously, and that its gross and harmful exaggerations have to be recorded against those who have stopped at nothing to vilify a steady, peace-loving, and thrifty section of Empire-builders,

"However, to take the arguments urged by the writer of the article under comment, it is stated that so far as the Natal general dealers are concerned, they cater for more than the Indian community. Granted—but what of that? Who are their *clientèle*? It is found that Indian petty traders deal with poor whites who, otherwise, would be unable often to procure even necessaries, let alone luxuries. Again, the Indian trader has dealings, often on a considerable scale, with natives. The native is unable to pay much for the commodities of which he is in need; he is a hard bargainer, and if he cannot get what he requires at the price that he is willing to pay, he goes without. Now, from the point of view of the South African colonist, the man who is able to create a demand for the products of civilization amongst the natives, and so offers inducements to them to hire their services out for a longer period, is performing a public service, and is deserving of the title rather of a benefactor of, than that of a danger to, the white community. There is a great deal of mystery about that blessed word 'competition.' Under existing economic conditions, competition is the very breath of trade. But there is competition and competition, and the burden of the charge made against the British-Indian is that his is unfair competition—a charge which, we maintain, has never yet been borne out. The head and forefront of our offending is not that we unfairly compete, but that we are foreigners, that our colour is brown, and that our habits are not similar to those which tradition and custom have imposed upon Europeans. Where the Indian trader is to be found, he supplies a much-needed demand, else should we never hear the constantly reiterated charge of undue competition. He trades often on a most diminutive scale, and the mere fact that he holds a general dealer's licence does not necessarily make him a general dealer. Big words are often used to exaggerate the importance of small things, and we are sure that, were the situation to be investigated in a spirit where humour could have free play, there would be many a hearty laugh at the expense of those who have unconsciously been led astray by a term that seems to include men whose wealth approximated to that of Crœsus rather than to that of the picker up of unconsidered trifles.

"Our remarks apply as much to the Transvaal as to Natal. How can there possibly be over-competition of Indians in a town such as Potchefstroom, where there are actually fewer Indians and more European traders than before the war? When we consider that, to-day, the Indian population of the Transvaal is considerably less than it was before the war, whilst the European population has increased beyond belief during that same period, it is obvious that the outcry against British-Indians is a false and a shallow one, and one, moreover, that is only urged by interested parties who desire to serve their own ends, and who are supported by men ever ready to be 'taken in' by a statement sufficiently often repeated. When we come to the Cape Colony, where one of the Indian storekeepers is stated to control no less than twenty-nine separate shops, we are tempted to search the records of the 'National' Convention for authority for this statement of 'fact,' or, on the other hand, to inquire how much larger than match-boxes those stores are! Truly, we are come to a sorry pass when such 'terminological inexactitude' is resorted to. Compared with the bulk of internal and external trade done by the European population, that done by British-Indians is insignificant, whilst that of other Asiatics or so-called Asiatics, with whom we have no immediate concern, must be a negligible quantity. Let us consider the condition of affairs. In Natal, there exists an Immigration Restriction Law which does not recognize the great Indian languages. Result—large numbers of Indians are, even if they wished to enter the country, debarred from so doing. There is a General Dealers' Licences Act, which makes the Town Council, composed of the Indian trader's business rivals, the final court of appeal, a condition of affairs which would not be tolerated in the United Kindom or in any place in which considerations of justice reigned supreme. In the district of Vryheid, the unfortunate British-Indian is subject both to the harsh laws of Natal and those of the Transvaal. At the Cape, a similar Immigration Restriction Law obtains to that enforced in Natal, with the additional restriction that if an Indian's wife and family be not resident in the country, he is not regarded as being domiciled in the colony. In the Orange River Colony, no Indian is permitted to remain in the country, except in a servile capacity.

"And in the Transvaal, things are no better. A Peace Preservation Ordinance is wrongly forced from its real intention, and, for political purposes, is used in practice to prevent the entry of Indians, even when entitled to be in the country. Law 3 of 1885 prevents their holding land, and obliges traders to possess themselves of registration certificates. Numberless other restrictions are imposed, but what we have already shown demonstrates our point. The writer of the article urges moderation on both sides. We agree. Our moderation consists in this—British-Indians desire treatment as free men, not as pariahs. They ask for free entry, on equal terms with non-Indians, into the Colonies, freedom to trade, freedom from the galling insults and degradations imposed by Law 3 of 1885. On their side they are willing to abide by a general immigration restriction law, and the granting of licences by the Town Councils, subject to appeal to the Supreme Courts. Can they, in justice to their own cause, in justice to their children, in justice to the great heritage of Empire that has become theirs and which they have helped to purchase with their blood and treasure—can they ask less than this ? British-Indians demand no political rights. They ask for nothing in the shape of social equality. But they have a right to insist upon the bestowal upon them of their just civil rights and the withdrawal of restrictions and restraints which can only have the effect of perpetuating the feeling of bitterness that must inevitably arise under a sense of oppression and injustice. For British-Indians to ask less than this would be to proclaim themselves as deserving of all the cruel hardships and insults inflicted upon them."

APPENDIX III

THE WRONG POLICY—TWO "HARD CASES"

THE following extracts are two instances of the wrong policy to pursue against the Asiatic—the policy which irritates and does not the slightest good. They explain themselves :—

THE JAPANESE MERCHANT

The following is a leading article from the *Transvaal Leader*, November 29, 1905 :—

"FOR SHAME"

"A letter appeared in the *Star* of yesterday from Mr. Nomura, one of the leading merchants of Japan, which raises questions of such importance that we cannot refrain from commenting on it. Mr. Nomura, who has exhibited various articles in European, American, and Australian cities, came to South Africa on the same errand. He had a passport signed by the Japanese Minister of Foreign Affairs, and endorsed by the British Consul at Kobe, and was further armed with credentials from the Commercial and Industrial departments of his Government. On arrival at Durban he sent forward his goods to Johannesburg, where they have been much admired. He himself, however, was detained at Durban, where his finger-prints were taken, pending the receipt of a permit to enter the Transvaal. After six weeks the Permit Office of the Transvaal refused him permission to enter the Transvaal.

"This is Mr. Nomura's plain story, and we venture to say that it is one which should make every inhabitant of this colony blush with shame. A gentleman of high standing in his own country, the reputation of whose firm is world-wide, vouched for by his own Government and by the British Consul in his native town, comes to this country on a most legitimate and proper errand, only to be subjected to indignity and to be refused admission. The officials of the Permit Office will have to explain why a delay of six weeks occurred before they could make up what they are pleased to call their minds, but this slothfulness, scandalous as it is, is only the smallest scandal connected with this affair.

"We can see every day proofs of the utter incompetence of the Permit Office to perform its duties. People of a low type are constantly admitted; notorious criminals find no difficulty in entering the Transvaal, though a reference to the Criminal Investigation Department would be both easy and efficacious. From time to time a few wretched Asiatics are sent over the border, living examples of the vigilance of the Permit Office, while depravity struts through the town hall-marked by its approval. And then comes a gentleman of character and position applying for a pass to pay a flying visit to Johannesburg on business, only to be insulted and refused. The officials of the Permit Office have only themselves to thank if nasty things are said, and if ugly rumours gain credence as to their methods and motives of selection. This case, however, will not be entirely without advantage if it leads people to ask whether it is worth while to squander some thousands a year on an office which is worse than useless. Something might be said for it if it protected us from the incursions of paupers, of men of criminal antecedents, and of men who live on a traffic which we need not specify, but nothing is to be said for it when it allows the town to be flooded with these, and then, to justify its existence, perpetrates an act of gross injustice, and one which might easily have serious international results.

"The Japanese are a highly civilized people who have set an example of business aptitude, of organizing ability, and of patriotic devotion to the whole world. They are the allies of Great Britain, whose interests in the East they are pledged to maintain, as we are pledged to defend theirs. The nation is proud to honour them. At the Trafalgar celebration nothing was more prized than the message from Admiral Togo, whom the United Kingdom will receive next year with a respect and admiration which would be accorded to few white men. Though, indeed, we are almost ashamed to allude to questions of colour in this connection. It may be quite right—we think it is—for a country to reserve the right of saying under what conditions foreigners may reside and trade within its borders, and of regulating their admission, but that does not hinge entirely on colour, and is at all events utterly distinct from the question of a temporary visit. Moreover, it is only bigotry or ignorance which can refuse to recognize those distinctions of position, character, and education, which are as patent and well-marked in Oriental countries as in Europe. Mr. Seddon, indeed, proposes to exclude Japanese from New Zealand, but, without any disrespect to that fine Colony, we venture to claim a wider and more cosmopolitan outlook for the inhabitants of the Transvaal. Even exclusive Australia has admitted Mr. Nomura, and yet the Transvaal is dragged by some incompetent officials into the absurd position of keeping him out. Mr. Nomura is about to appeal to the British Foreign Office, and we most sincerely hope that his representations may be successful. In the meantime we desire to emphatically condemn the action of the Permit authorities, to apologize for the indignities which have been put upon this Japanese gentleman, and to express our abhorrence of the whole wretched affair."

THE INDIAN STUDENT

The following is a leading article from the *Rand Daily Mail* of April 17, 1906:—

"It will probably seem curious to many people that a

man who claims to be a Portuguese subject should be granted a privilege which Transvaal officialdom has refused to the very same man when he was supposed to be a British subject. But this is what happened in the case of Mr. Suliman Manga, which has been taken up by *Indian Opinion;* and as a certain principle is involved it is well to note the mysterious workings of the official mind. Briefly the facts are these. Mr. Manga, who is the son of a well-known Indian at Delagoa Bay, is a member of the Middle Temple. Returning from his legal studies in England, he landed at Durban, and, desiring to visit his parents at Lourenco Marques, applied for a temporary permit to pass through the Transvaal on his way there. The Transvaal officials refused to grant it, and an application to the Colonial Secretary was also answered in the negative. Mr. Manga thereupon went to Delagoa by sea, but, being still anxious to see the Transvaal, renewed his request to the Protector of Asiatics there. For the third time he met with a refusal, and, as in the other instances, he was not informed what precise danger would threaten the Transvaal were he to be within its borders even for a day or two. But then Mr. Manga remembered that he was a native of Portuguese territory in India, and, claiming to be a Portuguese subject, he appealed to the Portuguese Government. Then the *Open Sesame* was discovered. The British Consul at Delagoa promptly granted a temporary permit, and the man who was rejected with contemptuous silence as a subject of the British Empire crossed the Transvaal border as a citizen of Portugal. Verily the ways of officialdom are remarkable.

"Now we object to an influx of Asiatics into the Transvaal as much as the most vigorous orator at the National Convention. No one could hold more strongly than we do to the conviction that the Transvaal can be made in a large measure a white man's country. No one would more emphatically protest against Asiatic labour being imported save under the Labour Importation Ordinance; no one could desire a more formidable barrier to the indiscriminate immigration of Asiatics than the one we should be prepared to erect. But it is quite another thing to approve of the purblind ineptitude displayed by officialdom in the case of Mr. Manga. The refusal to allow Mr. Nomura, the Japanese merchant, to enter the colony was a brilliant effort of administrative foresight compared to the rejection of Mr. Manga one day as a British subject and his admittance the next as a Portuguese. Mr. Nomura had at least the desire to trade. Mr. Manga had nothing to sell; he would compete with no man; all he wanted was to pass through the Transvaal on his way to visit his relations at Delagoa Bay. He asked only for a temporary permit. Had it been broken we will give the Transvaal authorities credit for sufficient intelligence to have sooner or later discovered the fact. But there was not the faintest ground for suspecting that the temporary character of the permit would not be strictly observed. The refusal was simply an instance of that gratuitous stupidity which has more than once affected Transvaal officials when dealing with Asiatics. Lord Milner was in a prophetic mood when, addressing the first Municipal Congress three years ago, he said: 'The greatest danger of every sound policy is its exaggeration and its travesty.' Lord Selborne has more than once expressed regret that it should be necessary to curtail the movements of British-Indian subjects in a British colony. That the necessity does arise, and must be provided for, we agree. That the necessity involves the refusal of the grant of a temporary permit to an Indian lawyer to cross through the Transvaal we cannot admit. The colony cannot be made into a twentieth century Forbidden Land. Maintain the vital principle by all means, even if it is necessary to use the language used by Australia twenty years ago. Refuse to allow fresh immigrants to enter and compete with the white population. But in the name of commonsense do not let us make the Transvaal a laughing-stock of the world by comic opera methods such as have been displayed by the Permit Office in the case of Mr. Manga. Seven years ago Lord Lansdowne, speaking of British-Indian disabilities in the Transvaal, said: 'What do you imagine would be the effect produced in India when these poor people return to their country to report to their friends that the Government of the Empress, so mighty and irresistible in India, with its population of 300,000,000, is powerless to secure redress at the hands of a small South African State?' What will be 'the effect produced in India' to-day if it becomes known that a native of Portuguese Goa is treated in a British colony with a consideration which is denied him when he says he is a subject of the British-Indian Empire? Here at least is an instance of that 'exaggeration' and 'travesty' which Lord Milner warned the colony against as the greatest danger of a sound Asiatic restriction policy."

At Volksrust the magistrate fined an Indian boy under eleven years of age £50, or three months' imprisonment, for being in the Transvaal without a permit. The Supreme Court quashed the conviction.

At the same Court an Indian woman was dragged from her husband's side and ordered to leave the Colony within seven hours. She refused to go, and the prosecution against her was ordered to be withdrawn.

APPENDIX IV

THE ASIATIC POPULATION OF NATAL

THE following return shows the distribution of the "Europeans or Whites" and the "Indians and Asiatics" in Natal (the Asiatics other than Indians only number a few score) :—

Magisterial Division or Centre.	Europeans or Whites.		Indians and Asiatics.	
	Males.	Females.	Males.	Females.
Klip River	632	475	1,044	362
Lion's River	900	664	897	381
Ixopo	479	397	102	36
*Alexandra County	542	411	3,986	2,368
Upper Umkomanzi	517	433	469	176
Newcastle	1,375	956	1,051	444
Mpendhle	312	202	167	68
Dundee	1,129	831	1,682	310
[1] Inanda	828	730	12,636	8,838
[1] Lower Tugela	523	434	6,274	4,754
Bergville	293	235	77	34
Estcourt	1,497	1,160	988	333
Mapumulo	33	19	4	—
Umgeni	617	484	1,245	719
New Hanover	859	777	648	247
Umlazi	3,359	2,885	13,403	9,595
Alfred County	274	208	43	8
Camperdown	508	442	589	224

[1] Coast districts.

Magisterial Division or Centre.	Europeans or Whites.		Indians and Asiatics.	
	Males.	Females.	Males.	Females.
Umvoti County	569	410	217	90
Ndwedwe	17	12	1	—
Utrecht	1,033	909	1	—
Krantyzop	194	154	26	10
[1] Umzimkulu	540	372	950	438
Umsinga	150	110	34	28
Vryheid	1,533	1,309	4	—
Paulpietersburg	493	477	—	—
Weenen County	437	291	52	11
Polela	363	237	117	109
Underberg	216	157	58	12
Estowe, Zululand	325	250	47	33
N'qutu, ,,	79	67	1	—
Nkandhla, ,,	96	42	—	—
Emtomjaneni, ,,	210	145	1	—
Ndwandwe, ,,	51	24	—	—
[1] Umfolosi, ,,	32	11	4	1
[1] Umbombo, ,,	17	6	2	—
Hlabisa, ,,	66	27	5	—
[1] Imgwavuma, ,,	24	7	—	—
[1] Umlalazi, ,,	96	67	18	8
Mahlabatini, ,,	29	22	—	—
Municipality of Pietermaritzburg	8,134	6,952	3,588	1,692
[1] ,, ,, Durban	18,777	12,525	10,509	5,122
,, ,, Ladysmith	1,284	985	781	355
,, ,, Newcastle	614	552	348	167
,, ,, Dundee	685	627	313	95
*Local Board, Verulam	189	174	448	252
,, ,, Greytown	545	572	191	80
,, ,, Utrecht	296	246	—	—
,, ,, Vryheid	779	565	31	13

[1] Coast districts.

The figures are summarized thus : —

RURAL DISTRICTS

	Males.	Females.
Europeans or Whites	21,247	16,849
Indians and Asiatics	46,903	29,637

URBAN DISTRICTS

	Males.	Females.
Europeans or Whites	35,511	23,502
Indians and Asiatics	16,594	7,784

APPENDIX V

LORD MILNER AND SIR ARTHUR LAWLEY

Two of the best written and most important official despatches on the Asiatic question—or in this particular case the British-Indian question—were written by Lord Milner, High Commissioner of South Africa and Governor of the Transvaal, and Sir Arthur Lawley, Lieut.-Governor of the Transvaal (now Governor of Madras), in reply to Sir M. M. Bhownaggree's letter to the Colonial Secretary. These two despatches sum up the Asiatic problem very fairly. They are as follows:—

GOVERNOR VISCOUNT MILNER TO MR. LYTTELTON

(*Received May* 7, 1904.)

GOVERNOR'S OFFICE, JOHANNESBURG,
April 18, 1904.

SIR,

I have the honour to enclose a despatch from the Lieutenant-Governor of the Transvaal, in whch he reviews the whole position as regards British-Indians. Of course, the proposed legislation on this subject will not apply to British Indians only, but to Asiatics generally. At the same time it is the fact that the majority of Asiatics in this Colony are British subjects from India, and it is owing to this fact that the Government of the Transvaal is placed in a position of peculiar embarrassment in dealing with the Asiatic question.

Sir Arthur Lawley has stated so fully the extent and the causes of the strong anti-Asiatic feeling among the European population of this Colony, that I need not myself dwell upon that factor in the problem. I can only say that I agree with Sir Arthur Lawley's statements with regard to it, and believe that he has not in any way exaggerated the caution with which, in view of this feeling, it behoves the Government to approach legislation on the subject of the status of Asiatics.

I must frankly confess that I am greatly disappointed with the position in which I find myself placed in this matter. I have always felt, as strongly as any one, the necessity of preventing an indiscriminate influx of Asiatics into this Colony, and I agree with all that Sir Arthur Lawley says as to the danger to the white population, and indeed to the whole political position, which such an influx would involve. We need a great increase in the white population of the new Colonies, and it is obviously desirable that this increase should be mainly British. But it is just with the British townsman that the Asiatic trader, who has flooded Natal, and who would certainly flood the new Colonies if he were allowed to, most seriously competes. But while upholding the policy of restrictions on Asiatic immigration, I always hoped to be able to carry it out in a manner sufficiently considerate of the feelings of our Indian fellow-subjects, and of the difficulties of the British and Indian Governments in the matter, to mitigate, if not altogether to remove, the objections which any system of restriction was certain to excite. In particular, I thought it would be possible, by giving to Asiatics of a superior class, a special status, and treating them virtually like Europeans, to avoid, at any rate, the appearance of race legislation. I still believe that this would be the best course. I believe that if the European, and especially the British, population in this country could be induced to see the matter in a reasonable light, such a course would provide not, indeed, a perfect, but a fairly satisfactory, solution of the difficulty. It is not, in my opinion, an influx of Asiatics of the upper and middle classes (professional men and merchants as distinct from small traders) which really threatens this community. If by treating this class liberally, we could induce the Government of India to acquiesce in the virtual exclusion of the petty trader class, who are out of place here, and at the same time to agree to the introduction, under conditions ensuring their ultimate return to their native country, of Indian labourers, whom we greatly need, and who could earn in this country such wages as they can obtain nowhere else in the world, I believe that the arrangement would be beneficial both to the Transvaal and to India.

This view is consistent with the opinions which I hold on the coloured question generally. I think that to attempt to place coloured people on an equality with whites in South Africa is wholly impracticable, and that, moreover, it is in principle wrong. But I also hold that when a coloured man possesses a certain high grade of civilization, he ought to obtain what I may call "white privileges," irrespective of his colour. I have, on more than one occasion, given expression to these views. They are very unpopular in the Transvaal at the present time, but I do not despair of their ultimately prevailing.

For the present, however, there is no prospect whatever of their prevailing, certainly as far as Asiatics are concerned. There is, perhaps, more chance in the case of the coloured people of South African birth. And no doubt their claim is a stronger one, inasmuch as they are natives of the country, and have no choice but to live here, while the Asiatics are strangers forcing themselves upon a community reluctant to receive them. Be that as it may, I am satisfied that it would not be possible for the Lieutenant-Governor and the Executive Council of the Transvaal, in view of the almost unanimous opposition of the white population, to introduce legislation more favourable to Asiatics than that which is now proposed. This legislation does carry out, to a certain extent, the idea of creating a category of "exempted" Asiatics, *id est*, of relaxing, in the case of Asiatics of the better class, most of the personal restrictions imposed upon Asiatics generally. But it is very far from putting "exempted" Asiatics on the same level as Europeans, as personally I should like to put them, and as I at one time hoped, not only with the view of meeting the wishes of the Government of India, to be able to put them.

There is another respect, in which the proposed legislation with regard to Asiatics, as sketched by Sir Arthur Lawley, falls short of what I have, in previous communications, and notably in my telegram of the 1st February, indicated as being the length to which the Transvaal Government was prepared to go in meeting the wishes of the Indian Government. I refer to the question of allowing Indian as well as European languages to be used in the education test, to which would-be immigrants are to be subjected. Sir Arthur Lawley and the Executive Council now think, and I am disposed, on reconsideration of the point, to agree with them, that, in making this concession, we should be going too far. I am not sure that it would not result in the admission of a very large number of Asiatics of the class whom it is desirable, as far as possible, to exclude. But apart from that, there is another and a very serious difficulty, which I admit did not occur to me in the first instance, but which was suggested by your telegram of the 7th March,[1] and that is that, in admitting Indian languages, we should be departing most seriously from the provisions of the Immigration Laws of both the Cape Colony and Natal, and breaking down the principle of uniformity of action with regard to the immigration question between the different Colonies. This would, in my opinion, be a most serious evil. Moreover, we have, on many occasions, declared our intention of passing an Immigration Act framed on the same lines as those of the two self-governing Colonies. If the Government of the Transvaal were to introduce into the Legislative Council an Immigration Ordinance differing materially from those

[1] Not printed.

of the sister Colonies, and above all, differing from them in the direction of giving greater encouragement to Asiatic immigration, it would have to face such a storm, both in the Legislative Council and outside, as it has never had to face yet, even on this subject, and it could only carry the proposal, so to speak, at the point of the bayonet.

It is quite true that, in the present state of public feeling, any proposal whatever for dealing with the position of Asiatics, short of the absolute exclusion of future immigrants and the relegation of the Asiatics already in the country to bazaars selected for them by the local authorities, will meet with much opposition, and may have to be carried in the Legislative Council by the votes of the official members alone. But on such a question as that of dealing fairly with the Asiatics already here, I should not scruple to employ, though I should regret the necessity of employing, the official majority to vote down popular opposition. We are entitled to use that majority in order to enable us to carry on the ordinary work of Administration, and to ensure the safety and good government of the Colony as long as we are responsible for them. We are entitled to use it to fulfil our obligations, and to do justice to even the most unpopular section of the community. But when it comes to a question, not of some administrative act of immediate necessity, or of the fulfilment of a particular obligation, but of permanent and organic legislation, then I think that the principle, so often enunciated by His Majesty's Government, of dealing with the Transvaal, though a Crown Colony, as if it were self-governing, applies. That being so, while we should be justified in legislating, even contrary to public opinion, to protect the vested rights of Indians already here, we should not, in my judgment, be justified in regulating the Asiatic question, in so far as it is, *res integra,* in a manner opposed to the views of the vast majority of the European population. And certainly it requires no referendum to ascertain those views with regard to Asiatic immigration or the status of Asiatics. No doubt, even if this were a self-governing

Colony, His Majesty's Government would refuse assent, as it has done in the case of other self-governing Colonies, to legislation involving manifest injustice to any race of men or grossly conflicting with the principles of Imperial policy as regards His Majesty's British Indian subjects. But legislation, such as is now proposed by Sir Arthur Lawley and the Executive Council of the Transvaal, is yet not legislation which, if adopted by a self-governing Colony, His Majesty's Government would demur to. It is, indeed, far more favourable to the Indians than any legislation likely to be passed here when this Colony obtains responsible Government, though I believe, if passed now, no Ministry holding power under a system of responsible Government will care to interfere with it.

I ought, perhaps, to state definitely, though I think it is sufficiently clear from Sir Arthur Lawley's despatch that it is the intention of the Transvaal Government, if you approve, to introduce, in the forthcoming Session of the Legislative Council, two measures bearing on this subject:—

I. An Immigration Ordinance on the lines of the Acts passed in the Cape Colony and Natal. This Ordinance, though applying to immigrants generally, and not expressly directed against Asiatics, will, in practice, have the effect of limiting the influx of Asiatics of the lower class.

II. An Ordinance dealing with the status and privileges of Asiatics already resident in the country, or who may hereafter become resident here.

The provisions, which it is intended that this latter Ordinance should contain, are clearly laid down in the enclosed despatch from Sir Arthur Lawley.

The immediate object of my present communication is to ask whether His Majesty's Government would be prepared to approve of the Transvaal Government introducing legislation on these lines in the next Session of the Legislative Council, Whatever difference of opinion there may be with regard to this question, no one, who has been resident in this country during the last two years, would be inclined to doubt that some immediate settlement is absolutely necessary. The present uncertain condition of affairs is bad for everybody. It exasperates the European population against the Asiatics, while the Asiatics themselves are subject to the most harassing and unfair uncertainty as to their future prospects. The controversy has now lasted incessantly since the first establishment of British power in the Transvaal, and I have no hesitation in saying that every month that it lasts makes it more difficult for the Government to carry any measures which are even moderately favourable to the Asiatic population. No doubt the feeling against them has been greatly aggravated by the recent outbreak of plague in the coolie location in Johannesburg. Had that outbreak been of a more serious and protracted character, the position would have become very grave. I think it would have required a stern exercise of the powers of Government to prevent the white population, especially in the smaller country towns, from taking the law into their own hands, and attempting at once to force all Asiatics, regardless of social position or vested rights, into locations selected by the local authorities, which would, in many cases, have been wholly unsuitable for their reception. This fever of excitement is now subsiding, but the permanent effect of the plague outbreak in confirming the anti-Asiatic sentiment throughout the country cannot be ignored. Even before the plague broke out, the anti-Asiatic agitation was steadily gathering force. That agitation will, in my opinion, go on and grow more and more formidable unless the position is cleared up, as it only can be cleared up, by fresh legislation.

But while asking for the assent of His Majesty's Government to the proposed Ordinances, not because I think them good, but because I think them the best we can carry, and because any definite settlement of the question would be better than the present chaos, I can hardly expect that these measures will satisfy the Government of India. It is deeply to be deplored that the Government of India should refuse to permit its subjects of the labouring class to come to this country, where they might earn in a few years, and with a certainty of good treatment while here, wages which would relieve them from poverty for the rest of their lives. But if, in the opinion of the Government of India, it is impossible to allow coolie immigration into the Transvaal, unless the laws of the Transvaal with regard to Indians generally are framed in a liberal spirit, then I fear there is nothing for it but for us to renounce, for the time being, the hope of coolie immigration.

If my opinion could be expected to carry any weight with the rulers of India, I should strongly advise that, notwithstanding what they must consider the unsatisfactory character of our Asiatic legislation, they should, nevertheless, not prohibit the immigration of Indian coolies into this Colony. And I should do so on the ground that, while such immigration would benefit the coolies, the refusal to allow it could not possibly be of advantage to any other class of Indians. This, however, is only the expression of my personal views. I do not suppose that the Government of India is likely to share them. But, while regretting the probable failure of our attempts to meet the Government of India in the matter, I feel that, coolies or no coolies, it is necessary for the peace and good government of this Colony to get the question of the status of Asiatics settled without much further delay. And as the settlement now proposed by Sir Arthur Lawley is, in my opinion, the best we can arrive at without flying in the face of the whole white community, and causing a serious strain to the good relations of this Colony with the Mother Country, I strongly recommend His Majesty's Government to allow us to carry it into effect.

I have, etc.,

MILNER,

Governor.

LIEUTENANT-GOVERNOR, TRANSVAAL, TO GOVERNOR.

LIEUTENANT-GOVERNOR'S OFFICE, PRETORIA,

April 13, 1904.

MY LORD,

The necessity for introducing legislation with regard to the status of Asiatics, and particularly British Indians, residing in the Transvaal becomes more urgent every day. Two incidents have recently occurred which have an important bearing on the whole question.

Having decided that all Asiatic traders should be removed to bazaars set apart for them in the various towns, with the exception of those who had *bonâ fide* established businesses before the outbreak of war, the Government refused to issue licences to certain traders who had not complied with the condition of removal into a bazaar.

In so acting the Government relied on the provisions of Law No. 3 of 1885. The validity of their action has now been challenged, and a test case will shortly be brought into the Supreme Court to decide whether under that law the Government have power to prohibit trading and residence except in places pointed out by the Government.

I am advised by the Attorney-General that in his opinion the decision of the late High Court on this point will probably be reversed by the Supreme Court, and that it will be impossible for the Government to carry into effect the restrictions upon Asiatics in regard to trade and residence which they deem necessary.

The second incident which has brought the whole question into prominence is the outbreak of bubonic plague in the location set apart for coolies in Johannesburg.

The Government have already experienced the greatest difficulty in securing the assent of the local bodies in the various towns to the establishment of bazaars within the municipal area, and it has been necessary for them to override the prejudices of the local authorities, and insist that the sites for these bazaars should be easily accessible and suitable for trading purposes. The clearest indications are already apparent that, in consequence of the outbreak of plague in Johannesburg there will be most bitter opposition from the white residents to any settlement of the question which is not based on the location of Asiatics in bazaars outside the towns. What was before merely a difficulty has now, owing to the outbreak of the plague, become almost an impossibility.

Owing to these two incidents, the question has become intensely acute, and I would, therefore, urge upon Your Excellency the desirability of securing the consent of His Majesty's Government to the introduction during the next Session of the Legislative Council of a measure embodying the policy laid down by the Transvaal Government in Government Notice No. 356, of 1903,[1] and referred to in your despatch to the Right Honourable the Secretary of State of the 1st February, 1904.

The legislation which it is proposed to introduce would contain the following provisions in regard to Asiatics, which term is taken to include British Indians :—

1. It is proposed to exempt from the necessity of residing in a distinct Asiatic quarter those Asiatics who satisfy the Colonial Secretary that they are possessed of intellectual attainments, social qualities, and habits of life such as to fit them for a mode of living in accordance with European ideas.

Asiatics to whom such exemption is granted will have the right to live anywhere. If they come under the category of the next succeeding Section (2) they will be allowed to trade outside bazaars, but otherwise not.

They will be exempt from registration ; otherwise they will not be exempt from the existing disabilities on coloured people.

Servants of exempted Asiatics, will be allowed to live with their employers.

2. In regard to Asiatics already here, the vested interests

---

[1] Printed in [Cd. 1684].

of those who had established businesses here before the war will be recognized and licences will be renewed to trade under the same conditions during the residence in this Colony of the licensee ; that is to say, it is not proposed to disturb those traders who had been allowed to establish themselves here before the war.

3. With the two exceptions above enumerated all Asiatics living within muncipal boundaries will be required to live or trade within bazaars set aside for the purpose. All Asiatics will be prohibited from holding land outside bazaars, but this prohibition will not apply in respect of land which is now set aside, and used for religious purposes.

4. All Asiatics entering the Transvaal shall, unless specially exempted, take out a certificate of registration at a charge of £3.

5. It is not proposed to put any restriction upon the issue of hawkers' licences, provided that sanction is given to the introduction of an Ordinance which will limit as far as possible the immigration of this class of Asiatic.

I realize very fully that legislation of such a restrictive nature may not at first sight commend itself to His Majesty's Government, but the events of the past twelve months have convinced every member of the Executive Council that any modification of such restrictions as are now proposed can only be insisted on in the face of most strenuous opposition by the public of this Colony. The attitude of the Commercial Community in the Colony has been made evident by constant resolutions adopted by every Chamber of Commerce throughout the Transvaal. In the course of debates which took place in the Legislative Council on the question of the granting of the Municipal Franchise to British Indians, and again, on the question of the renewal of licences to British Indian traders, the non-official members were—with the exception of Mr. Hosken—unanimous in condemning any policy which did not impose severe restrictions on all Asiatics. The revelation of this strong feeling has impressed the Government with the hopelessness of securing the acquiescence of the public in any further concessions to the British Indian than are contained in Law 3 of 1885.

The case for the British Indians is fully stated in a letter addressed by Sir M. Bhownaggree to Mr. Chamberlain, dated the 15th September, 1903,[1] which will doubtless be before His Majesty's Government when this matter comes up for consideration.

It is I think desirable that if possible the sentiments of the white population in regard to this matter should at the same time be clearly understood. I have no hesitation in saying that in all towns in the Transvaal the Asiatic question overshadows all others, and I fear that unless we are able to reconcile the opinion in England with the opinion held in this country the Government will be landed in a serious deadlock.

I do not seek to justify the prejudices which exist; I merely desire to set them forth.

They cannot be ignored. They have got to be reckoned with.

It is true that the British Government have laid down :—

> "that there shall not be in the eye of the law any distinction or disqualification whatever founded on mere distinction of colour, origin, language, or creed,"

but the history of South Africa has been such as to set up an impassable barrier between the European and the coloured races. The introduction and establishment of a white race into this country has only been effected after constant warfare with savage tribes, who have from time to time rebelled against the dominion of the white man. These outbreaks have invariably been accompanied by murders and outrages of a revolting description, of which many men now living have been actual eye-witnesses. These episodes cannot be effaced from the memory of any

[1] Enclosure in No. 1.

South African, and have engendered a feeling of animosity against the coloured man which cannot be eradicated by legislation.

Of course, in theory, the white residents of South Africa should easily differentiate between the uncivilized negro of South Africa and the British Indian, who has always been a temperate, law-abiding, citizen, but in the mind of the average Colonial, and particularly of the Dutch, a man is either a "white man" or a "coloured man," and the nicer distinctions of racial origin are completely lost sight of.

Under the old Grondwet the line was distinctly drawn between coloured and white. It is there stated there shall be no equality berween coloured and white, and though in the eye of the law they are equal, there is not in this country one man in a hundred who would agree to recognize the coloured man as capable of admission to the same social standard as the white.

I do not urge that these sentiments are reasonable, but they imbue the mind of every South African, and find expression in the universal cry of "A white man's country." The result of any attempt to ignore them would be attended, I feel sure, with most deplorable results.

Sir M. Bhownaggree's argument is to the effect that England has bound herself by explicit and repeated promises to place her Asiatic subjects on a footing of equality with British subjects throughout the Empire; that in the Transvaal such equal rights have been denied by the jealousy of European rivals, and that the Imperial Government is bound to intervene to redeem its pledges. Such a view might easily become impressed upon the minds of the English Public, but the consequence of an attempt to enforce it in this country would, in my opinion, be disastrous. Trade jealousy undoubtedly exists, but it is really prompted by the instinct of self-preservation in the minds of the European trading community. The problem does not begin and end with a shopkeeper's quarrel, but is more far-reaching than the questions whether this country shall be governed by Englishmen or Boers, or whether its mines shall be worked by Kaffirs or Chinese.

Sir M. Bhownaggree's argument is almost entirely historical, and he begins by reciting certain specific undertakings given in this country and elsewhere. When bringing the Indian Peninsula under the sovereignty of the British Crown, the Imperial Government pledged itself to make no distinction in law either in favour of or against any race or colour.

In the Proclamation of 1843, preliminary to the annexation of Natal, the same principle was expressly embodied.

There would have been no difficulty in multiplying instances of such declarations. The British Government enforced the observance of these principles upon the late Republican Government of the Transvaal, and so endorsed their promises by action.

In considering the position in which we are placed to-day we must remember not only the state of opinion which existed in the earlier half of the nineteenth century on the subject of racial equality, but also the events which have happened since. Pledges such as those contained in the proclamation of Sir Charles Napier were made at a time when large sections of the British nation had not come into touch with coloured races as they have to-day. It was commonly supposed that all races irrespective of race or colour were capable of the same civilization, and under this idea pledges were then made which the British Government has since struggled in the face of insuperable difficulties to carry out.

It was in accordance with this policy that the British Government resisted by every means in its power the imposition by the Transvaal Republic of restrictions upon British Asiatics. The British Government were merely adopting the policy which, as a matter of course, they would have adopted in any country where the rights of British subjects were being overridden, but I do not think that the consequences which must ultimately result from such a policy were realized at that time. To-day, the Government cannot fail to perceive the effects on the social composition of the country, which have already resulted from the concessions made to British Indians in the past, or to see clearly what will be the consequence of making still further concessions. The nature of these consequences may be learned by examining three typical examples—Johannesburg, Pietersburg, and Natal.

In these three instances the growth of the Indian population has been very different in proportion to the difference of the facilities afforded them. In the Transvaal the Republican Government were able to obey in some degree the instincts which prompt a Colonial population to check Indian immigration in spite of external pressure from the Imperial Government. But in this country, unlike countries where governments are more firmly established, law was strongly or weakly administered in proportion to the pressure which the local European population were able to apply. In Johannesburg there existed a strong commercial community with a well-organized Chamber of Commerce, and a class of customers whose standard of living is exceptionally high. In this town, therefore, Indians, though numerous, never became a very important element in the population. In the centre of the town there exist indeed a few Indian shops, but the great bulk of the Asiatic population confines itself to hawking vegetables and conducting a pedlar's trade amongst the Kaffirs on the mines. The general aspect of the town is that of a European community, and would remind the visitor more of London or Birmingham than of Cairo or Bombay. But in a remote community like Pietersburg, the case is very different. While the town supports a few substantial wholesale merchants almost the entire retail trade is in the hands of Indians. There are a few large stores belonging to European merchants which are the retail depôts of wholesale establishments. In addition to these there is one retail store in the hands of a small English trader. With these exceptions, and leaving aside hairdressers, chemists, and shops of a special nature, the whole of the retail trade round the square is in the hands of the Indians. In fact, the white men supported by the trade carried on round the Market Square in Pietersburg are numerically in the minority. The town from a commercial point of view has a hybrid appearance, the Indian element being rather more prominent than the European. But the most serious feature in this town is the increasing predominance of the Indians. A long list might be furnished of small white traders who once had stores round the Square, and have now been crushed out of existence. The total white population of Pietersburg is estimated at 1,684. The registers of the Asiatic Department show no less than 135 Indians almost entirely adult males, and practically all engaged in the business of store-keeping.

Sir M. Bhownaggree is evidently writing in ignorance of the existing circumstances of urban life outside Johannesburg and Pretoria when, in Section 18 of his letter to Mr. Chamberlain, he states that if the Franchise were granted with educational restrictions :—

> "there is not the shadow of a shade of fear of Indians dominating the elections or being sufficiently strong to turn the scale between rival parties in the Municipalities."

To come now to Natal. In that Colony the presence of the Indian has had an even more injurious effect upon the growth of a European population than in such a town as Pietersburg. So prevalent is the Indian element in that country that the moment one crosses the Transvaal Border he loses the impression that he is travelling in a European country at all. Natal has an immense native population, which twenty years ago was served in the way of trade only by Europeans. Traders of this class formed an important element in the white population of Natal. To-day this class of trader has vanished altogether, and their business is now entirely in the hands of Asiatics. I hope to be able to furnish tabulated information, which will give clear evidence of the effect which Indian immigration is having upon the development of the population.

The population of the South African Colonies may be divided into three classes. There is, first of all, the class engaged in official and professional work, and in the conduct of large undertakings. In this sphere the European will always remain supreme; it is, nevertheless, open to invasion by Asiatics. On a level with those, but in a category apart, are the farmers, almost entirely Dutch in nationality, whose sphere is unaffected by Asiatic competition. Secondly, there is the class of retail traders, and small cultivators or market-gardeners. It is quite possible for the Asiatic to exclude the European from this sphere altogether. Again, on a level with this second class, but quite apart from it, are the skilled tradesmen and mechanics, whose place might be taken by Asiatics, but who can probably be trusted by combination to maintain their ground. Thirdly, there is the class of unskilled labourers. This consists exclusively of Kaffirs whose insufficient number it is now proposed to supplement by indentured Chinese coolies. For the present, if not permanently, the white man steadily refuses to share this sphere with the Kaffir races. The statesman would be more than sanguine who expected to find room in this third division for the expansion of a white population. All we can say with certainty is that the numbers which can be maintained in the first two classes are dependent almost entirely on the numbers obtainable for the third class. The direct practical and immediate way to make room for white men in this country is by additions to the labouring classes, which is the necessary foundation upon which the superstructure of the other two classes can be built. As you enlarge these foundations so the two other classes will be enlarged automatically, but not in the same ratio, for the second and larger class will increase much more rapidly than the first.

Assuming, therefore, that the first duty of statesmen in this country is to multiply homes for white men, there is every justification for the enlargement of the labouring class by the introduction of Asiatics, provided the limitation of their sphere of work to that of unskilled labour is maintained. But it is very difficult to prove that the admission of Asiatics of the second class enlarges in other directions the sphere for white men to a degree which compensates for such admission. It may lead to a slight reduction in the cost of living, and thence to a certain enlargement of the mechanic class, but no new sphere for white men is created, which at all corresponds to the space which is filled up by the intrusion of the Asiatic into the sphere of commerce and agriculture. The nett result will be that to which Natal is approximating, where for 73,000 whites you have a population of 80,000 Indians, and where white men as small cultivators and retail traders have been well-nigh eliminated.

Sir M. Bhownaggree regards as most unfortunate the description of Indians of this country as "Asiatics of a low type." I have appended to this memorandum a recent correspondence in which Indian writers themselves lend colour to this observation. It is evident that it is not the Secretary of State who has been misinformed by Your Excellency, but Sir M. Bhownaggree who has been misinformed by his local correspondent. He remarks for instance that Dr. Porter's evidence as to the insanitary condition of the coolie location, and as to the danger of an outbreak of plague from that quarter :—

> "was controverted by (Dr. F. P. Marais and Dr. Johnson) medical men of at least equal authority, and of larger South African experience."

Dr. Porter's opinion was supported by the Medical Officer of Health for the Transvaal, the Medical Officer of Health for the Witwatersrand, and Dr. Murray, a medical man of long South African experience. Dr. Johnson definitely committed himself to the opinion that plague was not likely to break out in the location (see questions 6775 and 6776 of the Johannesburg Insanitary Area Commission Report). The present outbreak of plague originated in that location. Dr. Marais, on the other hand, steadily refused to commit himself to any such opinion, and the last two weeks have appended a tragic commentary to his caution on this point. After devoted attendance on supposed cases of pneumonia in the location, Dr. Marais himself died of the same symptoms on the 18th March, the day before the outbreak was identified as Pneumonic Plague. Within a week his wife, three of his four children, and his attendant succumbed to the disease.

Again, Sir M. Bhownaggree has been led by a petition to which the signatures of forty Europeans are attached to question the belief that public opinion is intensely hostile to the Indian Community. The signatories to the petition are leading residents of Johannesburg; and while I do not question for one moment the genuine nature of their appeal, the fact must not be lost sight of that, as I have demonstrated above, the conditions of Johannesburg at the present time are such that the big Enropean firms can well ignore the competition of Asiatic traders, and are in quite a different position from that of the European trader in the smaller towns. The difficulties experienced by the Colonial Secretary in establishing Asiatic Bazaars within reasonable distance of these towns in the face of strenuous opposition from their inhabitants point to the fact that Sir M. Bhownaggree has been strangely misinformed.

In my opinion we are face to face with a most difficult problem of modern civilization. The British Empire is now so extended as to include countries typical of every climate; it contains large tropical tracts, some, like India, thickly peopled, others, like Central Africa, almost destitute of population, both alike incapable of becoming the permanent home of a white nation. It likewise happens to contain a certain principal share of the temperate countries still open for settlement by European races. India belongs to the first class, and is a country in which the European leads a purely exotic existence. The European element as compared numerically to the native can never be otherwise than insignificant, and must always be confined to the official and military classes, and the higher branches of commerce and industry. In any other branch there never was and never will be any question of the European ousting the native. India has in her climate a protection more permanent and more effective against social invasion than any act of alien immigration could ever afford her.

But South Africa is one of the countries inhabitable alike by Europeans and Asiatics, and it is difficult to conceive any question at the present moment more momentous than the struggle between East and West for the inheritance of these semi-vacant territories. Promises have been made without knowledge or perception of the consequence involved in their fulfilment.

If the redemption of the pledges upon which Sir M. Bhownaggree depends both in letter and spirit means that in fifty or a hundred years this country will have fallen to the inheritance of the Eastern instead of Western populations, then from the point of view of civilization they must be numbered among promises which it is a greater crime to keep than to break. As India is protected by her climate against Europeans, so England is protected by the same agency against the invasion of the Asiatic, to which this country is subject. But if it were not so would the faith of these pledges be held to entitle the Indian shopkeeper to eliminate from English society the small shopkeeper and farmer? They would be held by English statesmen to be no more sacred than a promise which inadvertently committed a man to suicide. It was precisely this feeling which the anti-Chinese agitation aroused. The English electorate then showed themselves sufficiently strenuous for the exclusion of Asiatics who would reduce, it was thought, the market for white labour.

I have not touched upon the sanitary dangers arising from the presence of an Asiatic population, except to correct Sir M. Bhownaggree's statement. I have preferred to place the matter upon what I regard as its true footing. The Europeans who form the Commercial Community of this country are struggling for continued existence which is threatened by an influx of Asiatics. Owing to past events, vested interests have been acquired, which it is impossible for the Government of the Transvaal to ignore, but if this country in the future is to be a sphere for the development of an English population, the principles of our Asiatic policy must in my opinion be such as make the granting of traders' licences subject to the conditions enumerated above, and to control the future immigration of Asiatics by a law similar to that of Cape Colony and Natal. In considering the provisions restricting the immigration of aliens, it is obvious that as far as possible the legislation introduced by the various Colonies should be uniform. Cape Colony and Natal would have a legitimate grievance against the Transvaal if the laws in force in the latter Colony were less stringent than those in force in the former. If such were the case it would be quite easy for immigrants to enter the Transvaal viâ Delagoa Bay, and to make their way into the neighbouring Colonies. It is quite impossible to control ingress and egress from adjoining countries divided by a border line so extended as that which separates the Colonies of South Africa. I do not for one moment believe that the Legislatures of either Cape Colony or Natal will consent to the proposal to include the Indian language in the test to be applied to immigrants contained in the telegram from the Secretary of State of the 4th January, 1904.

Even if they are willing to do so, I am not, after mature consideration, prepared to submit such a proposal to the Legislative Council of the Transvaal although when it was originally suggested I offered no opposition thereto.

The episodes of the past few weeks have brought the Asiatic question into prominence, and I think that I am able to gauge with accuracy the feeling of the people of this country towards British Indians generally.

The outbreak of plague has demonstrated the bias of the European population, but I base my judgment rather on the exhibition of public feeling recently manifested in the Legislative Council, in the discussions of every Chamber of Commerce, and by the whole body of the public at the time when the Government undertook the task of selecting sites for bazaars. The British Indian Association maintains that these sites are quite unsuitable, but they have, in my opinion, overstated their case.

The objections raised by the townspeople have been also unreasonable.

I think that the selections have been well made.

Speaking generally I am convinced that a *modus vivendi* is only possible by a compromise, and that the basis of a compromise which will be acceptable to the Europeans of the Transvaal must be to treat fairly those Indians who have been allowed to come into the country, and to let any future immigrants know the disabilities under which they will be allowed to enter the Transvaal.

The prohibition which exists against the owning of land by British Indians is due to the same general instinct of self-preservation which has led to the protests against Indian traders by the Commercial Community. It is perfectly true that if it were possible for the Indians to acquire land and devote themselves to the cultivation of the soil, the necessaries of life in the way of garden produce which are now for the moment abnormally costly would be considerably cheapened, but the community would infinitely prefer to suffer a temporary disability in this respect than to see the establishment in their midst of a race of landowners whom they instinctively regard as aliens.

At the present time the market is glutted with farms for sale, and I have no doubt that if the restrictions now placed upon the acquisition of land by Indians were removed thousands of acres would at once pass into the hands of British Indians, many of whom have acquired immense wealth in trade both here and in Natal. The ignorant Dutch farmer is a credulous person, and just now is being crammed by unscrupulous people with the most absurd stories to the effect that the British Government is determined to wrest his land from him. The Fencing Act, the taking of a Census, the Stock Regulations, are interpreted as insidious means whereby the Government is seeking to acquire his farm. These stories are, of course, ridiculous, but they receive ready credence from the uneducated Boer, and they produce in his mind a sense of uneasiness, and a desire to "make hay while the sun shines," and dispose of his land on the first opportunity. The present would be a most unfortunate moment to bring into the land market an entirely new speculator, and it is our duty to save the farmers of the country from this danger.

For these reasons the Government deem it impossible to allow the indiscriminate acquisition of land by Indians, but they are prepared to allow Indians to hold land in bazaars or any other areas set apart for Asiatics. It would, moreover, be only reasonable to remove the vexatious provision of the existing law, by which Indians are prohibited from holding in their own name land devoted to religious purposes.

I have endeavoured to set forth clearly what I believe to be the true feeling of the general public in regard to this question as well as to give an outline of the legislation which we propose to introduce during the next Session of the Legislative Council. It embodies the policy contained in Government Notice No. 356, of 1903, to which this Government has steadily adhered. As I have already stated, I anticipate that the proposed restrictions on British Indians may appear to His Majesty's Government to be somewhat severe, but I am quite certain that we shall have the greatest difficulty in carrying in the Legislative Council even such a measure as I have described. There is no mistaking the feeling of the public on this question, and I am confident that great pressure will be put upon the Government to impose still further restrictions than those at present proposed, but it would be most unfortunate if we were after meeting with strenuous opposition to pass any measure in the Legislative Council which might afterwards fail to receive the approval of the Secretary of State.

Some legislative measure is urgently necessary, and I therefore earnestly hope that we may be informed with the least possible delay whether the Secretary of State will now give his approval to the introduction of legislation containing the provisions which I have enumerated above.

I have, etc.,

ARTHUR LAWLEY,

Lieutenant-Governor.

His Excellency

The Right Honourable Viscount Milner,

P.C., G.C.B., G.C.M.G., etc., etc.,

Johannesburg.

APPENDIX VI

LORD ELGIN AND THE TRANSVAAL INDIANS

THE following is a verbatim official report of the deputation of the Transvaal British Indian Association to Lord Elgin, Secretary of State for the Colonies, on November 8, 1906.

The Deputation consisted of the following gentlemen :—

LORD STANLEY of Alderley.
MR. H. O. ALLY } Delegates from the
MR. GANDHI } Transvaal.
SIR LEPEL GRIFFIN.
MR. J. D. REES, C.I.E., M.P.
SIR GEORGE BIRDWOOD, K.C.S.I.
SIR HENRY COTTON, K.C.S.I., M.P.
MR. NAOROJI.
SIR M. M. BHOWNAGGREE, K.C.I.E.
MR. AMIR ALI.
MR. HAROLD COX, M.P.
MR. THORNTON, C.S.I.

THE EARL OF ELGIN : I should like to say, gentlemen, that I made this interview a private one because I thought, from experience of other meetings of the same sort, we should be better able to discuss the matter friendlily across the table without the presence of public reporters ; at the same time, I am quite aware that the Deputation wish to go into matters of some detail, and therefore I have made arrangements for a note to be taken, so that anything which may be said shall be on record. Then I should like to say one other word. I recognize among the Deputation some of those with whom I have had the pleasure of working in India, and I hope they have explained to the Deputation, if it was necessary, that my sentiments would all be in favour of doing anything I could for the interest of the British Indians. (Hear, hear.)

SIR LEPEL GRIFFIN: My Lord, what you have just said makes my duty in introducing the Delegates more easy. We are very much obliged to your Lordship for admitting this deputation of men who are all known to you as gentlemen connected with India, who have been most of them in India themselves, and all are interested in India, and we are very glad, without any question of party feeling, because all sides are represented in this Deputation, to introduce to you the Delegates from South Africa, Mr. Gandhi who is, as your Lordship is aware, a barrister of the Inner Temple, and a man who, in the late Boer War, and in the late rising in Natal, has done most excellent work for the country in organizing ambulance corps and in other ways—he practises now in Johannesburg—and Mr. Ally, his colleague, who is the representative of the Mohammedan part of the Indian community in the Transvaal, a merchant of very good position, and the founder and, I believe, the Chairman of the Islamic Association in the Transvaal. To those gentlemen I propose to leave any details of the Ordinance which has now been passed and which we are about to ask His Majesty's Government to veto. But I would like to say a few words in explaining the matter before the Colonial Office, and I shall take up the time of your Lordship only for a few minutes. I have been asked to present this Deputation, principally, I fancy, because I happen to be the Chairman of the Council of the East India Association, of which your Lordship is a distinguished Vice-President, but the question which the East India Association has so often urged upon successive Colonial Secretaries and Secretaries for India and Viceroys of India, is not directly concerned in our presence here to-day. The bed-rock, as your Lordship is aware, of the East India Association's protest, that all well-conducted, loyal, and industrious British subjects, whatever their race or colour, should receive equal rights in all colonies of the British Empire; that is the bed-rock of justice which has always been refused in the past, but on which the East India Association, which is represented largely here to-day, begs to continue to rely, and from which it must continue to make its protest. That, my Lord, is not precisely the question which this Deputation desires to put forward this afternoon; they are not making any of those large claims which we have before made; they only ask that a certain Ordinance, applying to the Transvaal alone, may not receive the sanction of His Majesty's Government. A few words only are necessary on this point. During the Boer Government, the British Indians were treated with considerable harshness, but their immigration into the Transvaal was not prohibited, and with the exception of a fee for licence for adult traders, they were not interfered with. But their position was an exceedingly uncomfortable one, and many protests were raised, which, we understood, when the country fell into the hands of the English, would be redressed. So far from being redressed, their position is made worse, and the rules for registration and identification were made exceedingly more rigorous. The Ordinance, which has now been passed, makes, whatever people in South Africa may choose to say, their position infinitely worse and more degrading. It may be said that, in the Transvaal, these rules are for the benefit of the Indians, but the toad under the harrow knows where the harrow grips him, and the Indians in the Transvaal consider that the new regulations of this Ordinance are a grievance and an insult which is almost too grievous to be borne; and I for one most strongly support their claim and their protest. Under this Ordinance, every one in the Transvaal is exposed to the most rigorous investigation; the impressions of his fingers are to be recorded on every pass; no one is allowed in, man, woman, or child, without registration of so rigorous a character, that it has been unheard of in any civilized country within a recollection. Under this regulation, every

Indian in the Transvaal, whether an adult male, woman, or whether a child, and even babes in arms, will be obliged to be registered under such conditions as only ordinarily apply to convicts in a civilized country ; and evasion, or ignorance, or even forgetfulness on this point is punished by crushing fines, by imprisonment with hard labour, by expulsion, and by ruin. You, my Lord, who have been Viceroy of India, and whose sympathy is with the country, must know that legislation of this sort is unheard of under the British Flag ; indeed, to-day, in Europe I may say, without any exaggeration, that with the exception of the Russian legislation against the Jews, there is no legislation comparable to this on the Continent of Europe ; and in England, if we wanted a similar case, we should have to go back to the time of the Plantagenets. And against whom is this legislation directed ? Against the most orderly, honourable, industrious, temperate race in the world, people of our own stock and blood, with whom our language has, as a sister language, been connected. There is no occasion, in the presence of people connected with India, who know its history, to say what the Indian community is to-day ; it is almost an insult to refer to it. And by whom is this legislation instigated ? I am told, and I believe it, that it is not by the best part of the British Community in the Transvaal, who are, I believe, in favour of giving all reasonable privileges to British-Indian subjects ; it is by the alien foreign population in the Transvaal, who are, perhaps, to some extent inconvenienced by Indian traders, who are so very much more temperate and industrious than themselves. It does not come from the English. The legislation is prompted, and the prejudice against the Indians is encouraged, by the aliens, by Russian Jews, by Syrians, by German Jews, by every class of aliens, the very off-scourings of the international sewers of Europe. The English residents, against whom I do not wish to say one word of criticism, are a part, in my mind, of the Transvaal, but the Transvaal is only a colony by conquest, not by settlement, and it is the aliens who are opposed to this honourable Indian community. My Lord, I do not wish to take up more of your time, but what I wish to say is, that to-day we ask you, as representing His Majesty's Government, and as we know your sympathies are with the Indians over whom you have ruled with so much distinction, to procure the vetoing of this Ordinance. No large questions are brought before you to-day by this deputation. They are not asking for political rights; they are not asking for gratitude for their great and devoted services in the Transvaal War, where so many of them lost their lives in their devotion to England, doing as courageous work as any one of the members of the armies which were sent by England, by Australia, or by Canada. Those services have not been recognized; on the contrary, they have been ignored, and further burdens have been placed upon them. We ask for nothing to-day except the merest, barest justice. We ask that the whips which the Boers have inflicted upon us may not be changed into scorpions wielded by the British Government. I would say, in conclusion, that we hope everything from the present Government, and for this reason, that the grievances of the Chinese have received the utmost sympathy at the hands of the Government, but so far as this Deputation is concerned, the Chinese and other alien nations do not count. We ask, not for the Chinese, but for our own fellow-subjects, and we ask that justice, if not generosity, may be dealt out to them, and that your Lordship will save them from insult and oppression. It was at your Lordship's request that this deputation was a small one; it might have been indefinitely extended. This is a test-case—a question of going forward or going back. Your Lordship, as a past Viceroy of India, is aware that the attention of the whole of India, 300 millions of Indians, is intent to-day upon the decision which will be given in this test-case, and I beg your Lordship to think and to remember that, besides the Indians of Indian birth, against whom the insults of this Ordinance are directed, there are the whole body of Indian officials, to which I and most of the members of this Deputation belong, who are insulted with the natives of India. Is it not to be supposed that we, who have worked with, we who have governed, this province of India under your Lordship and under your predecessors and successors, have been governing degraded creatures who are placed lower even than the Zulus and Russian Jews? No my Lord! We trust to you to do what you can to defend the people whom you have governed so well. And I will beg you to excuse any exciting warmth in my way of speaking, because I assure you that any warmth in my words is very much exceeded by the feeling of shame and resentment which fills my heart at the way in which the British Indians of the Transvaal are treated to-day by the settlers (I will not call them colonists) of that country.

MR. GANDHI.

MR. GANDHI: Both Mr. Ally and I are very much obliged to your Lordship for giving us the opportunity of placing the British-Indian position before you. Supported though we are by distinguished Anglo-Indian friends and others, I feel that the task before Mr. Ally and myself is very difficult, because your Lordship, in reply to the cablegram sent to you through Lord Selborne, after the great Indian Mass Meeting in Johannesburg, was pleased to inform the British India Association that, although you would be pleased to give us every opportunity of stating our case, no good purpose was likely to be served, as your Lordship had approved of the principle of the Ordinance, in that it gave some measure of relief to the British-Indian community, though not as much as His Majesty's Government would desire. We, who are the men on the spot, and who are affected by the Ordinance in question, have ventured to think otherwise. We have felt that this Ordinance does not give us any relief whatsoever. It is a measure which places British Indians in a far worse position than before, and makes the lot of the British Indian well-nigh intolerable. Under the Ordinance, the British Indian is assumed to be a criminal. If a stranger, not knowing the circumstances of the Transvaal, were to read the Ordinance, he would have no hesitation in coming to the conclusion that an Ordinance of that nature, which carries so much penalties, and wounds the British-Indian community on all sides, must only apply to thieves or a gang of robbers. I venture, therefore, to think that, although Sir Lepel Griffin has used strong language in connexion with the Ordinance, he has not at all exaggerated, but every word of it is justified. At the same time, I beg to state that the Ordinance, as amended, does not apply to British-Indian females. The draft Ordinance undoubtedly applied to females also, but owing to the very strong protests made by the British-India Association, and by Mr. Ally separately, as Chairman of the Hamidia Islamic Society, pointing out the great violence that would have been done to female sanctity, if I may say so, the Ordinance was amended so as to take females out of its operation. But it applies to all adult males and even to children, in that the parents or guardians have to take out registration certificates for their children or wards, as the case may be. It is a fundamental maxim of the British law that every one is presumed to be innocent until he is found guilty, but the Ordinance reverses the process, brands every Indian as guilty, and leaves no room for him to prove his innocence. There is absolutely nothing proved against us, and yet every British Indian, no matter what his status is, is to be condemned as guilty, and not treated as an innocent man. My Lord, an Ordinance of this nature it is not possible for British Indians to reconcile themselves to. I do not know that such an Ordinance is applicable to free British subjects in any part of His Majesty's dominions. Moreover, what the Transvaal thinks to-day, the other colonies think to-morrow. When Lord Milner sprang his Bazaar Notice on British Indians, the whole of South Africa rang with the idea. The term " bazaar " is a misnomer ; it has been really applied to locations where trade is utterly impossible. However, a proposal was seriously made, after a bazaar notice, by the then Mayor of Durban, Mr. Ellis Brown, that Indians should be relegated to bazaars. There is not the slightest reason why this Ordinance also, if it ever becomes law, should not be copied by the other parts of South Africa. The position to-day in Natal is that even indentured Indians are not required to carry passes as contemplated by the Asiatic Law Amendment Ordinance; nor are there any penalties attached to the non-carrying of passes as are defined in the Ordinance under discussion. We have already shown, in our humble representation, that no relief has been granted by this Ordinance, because the remission of the £3 fee referred to by Mr. Duncan is quite illusory, because all we British Indians resident in the Transvaal, who are obliged to pay £3 under Law 3 of 1885, and those who, under Lord Selborne's promises are likely to be allowed to re-enter the Transvaal, have paid the £3 already. The authority to issue temporary permits is also superfluous, in that the Government have already exercised the power, and there are to-day in the Transvaal several Indians in possession of temporary permits. They are liable to be expelled from the Colony on the expiry of their permits. The relief under the Liquor Ordinance is, British Indians feel, a wanton insult. So much was this recognized by the local Government, that they immediately assured the Indians that it was not intended for British Indians at all, but for somebody else. We have no connexion with anybody else, and we have always endeavoured to show that the British Indians ought to be treated as British subjects, and ought not to be included with the general body of Asiatics with respect to whom there may be a need for some restrictions which ought not to apply to British Indians as British subjects. There remains one more sentiment, that is, in connexion with the land owned by the late Aboobaker. The land should belong to the heirs by right, but under the interpretation reluctantly put upon it by the Supreme Court, that it is only individual in character, and does not touch the community, the land cannot be transmitted to the heirs. The Ordinance is intended to rectify the error, but as I had the honour to represent the heirs, I ventured to think that even they would not consent to pay for getting this relief at the price, in the nature of the Ordinance for British Indians ; and certainly the Indian community can never exchange, for the relief given to the heirs of the land of Aboobaker, an Ordinance of this nature, which requires them to pay so great a price for what is really their own. So that under the Ordinance, in that respect again, there is absolutely no relief. As I said before, we shall be under the Ordinance branded as criminals. My Lord, the existing legislation is severe enough. I hold in my hands returns from the Court of the Magistrate at Volksrust. Over 150 successful prosecutions of Indians attempting to enter the Transvaal have taken place during the years 1905 and 1906. All these prosecutions, I venture to say, are by no means just. I venture to believe that if these prosecutions were gone into, you would see that some of them were absolutely groundless. So far as the question of identification is concerned, the present laws are quite enough. I produce to Your Lordship the Registration Certificate held by me, and it will show how complete it is to establish identification. The present law can hardly be called an amendment. I produce before Your Lordship a registration receipt held by my colleague, Mr. Ally, from the Transvaal Government. Your Lordship will see that it is merely a receipt for £3. The registration under the present Ordinance is of a different type. When Lord Milner wished to enforce Law 3 of 1885, he suggested new registration. We protested against it, but on his strong advice, as a voluntary act, we allowed ourselves to be newly registered ; and hence the form produced before Your Lordship. At the time the registration was undertaken, Lord Milner stated emphatically that it was a measure once for all, and that it would form a complete title to residence by those who had such registration certificates. Is all this now to be undone ? Your Lordship is doubtless aware of the Punia case, wherein a poor Indian woman, in the company of her husband, was torn away from her husband, and was ordered by the Magistrate to leave the country within seven hours. Fortunately relief was granted in the end, as the matter was taken up in time. A boy under eleven years was also arrested and sentenced to pay a fine of £30 or to go to gaol for three months, and at the end of it to leave the country. In this case again, the Supreme Court has been able to grant justice. The conviction was pronounced to be wholly bad, and Sir James Rose-Innes stated that the Administration would bring upon itself ridicule and contempt if such a policy was pursued. If the existing legislation is strong enough, and severe enough, to thus prosecute British Indians, is it not enough to keep out of the colony British Indians who may attempt fraudulently to enter it ? It has been stated that the reason for passing the Ordinance is that there is an unauthorized influx of British Indians into the Transvaal, on a wholesale scale, and that there is an attempt, on the part of the Indian community, to introduce Indians in such a manner. The last charge has been, times without number, repudiated by the Indian community, and the makers of the charge have been challenged to prove their statement. The first statement has also been denied. I ought to mention one thing also ; that is, the fourth resolution that was passed at the British-Indian Mass meeting. It was passed by the meeting solemnly, prayerfully, and in all humility, and the whole of that great meeting decided by that resolution that if this Ordinance ever came to be enforced and we did not get relief, the British Indians, rather than submit to the great degradation involved in it, would go to gaol—such was the intensity of the feeling aroused by the Ordinance. We have hitherto suffered much in the Transvaal and in other parts of South Africa ; but the hardship has been tolerable ; we have not considered it necessary to travel 6,000 miles to place the position before the Imperial Government. But the straining point has been reached by the Ordinance, and we felt that we should, in all humility, exhaust every resource, even to the extent of sending a deputation to wait on Your Lordship. The least, therefore, that in my humble opinion is due to the British-Indian community, is to appoint a Commission as suggested in the humble representation submitted to

Your Lordship. It is a time-honoured British custom that, whenever an important principle is involved, a Commission is appointed before a step is taken. The question of Alien Immigration into the United Kingdom is a parallel case. Charges somewhat similar to the charges against the Indian community were made against the aliens who enter the United Kingdom. There was also the question of adequacy of the existing legislation, and the necessity for further legislation. All these three points were referred to a Commission before any step was taken. I therefore venture to think that a Commission should be appointed, and the whole question thrashed out before any drastic measures are taken. I venture therefore to hope that Your Lordship will see your way to grant this small measure of relief to the British-Indian community.

MR. ALLY.

MR. H. O. ALLY: My Lord, we are very much obliged to you for the patient hearing Your Lordship is giving to the deputation. Mr. Gandhi has stated the case fully before Your Lordship, and I do not wish to add much to what has already been said. I am not a lawyer, but as a layman, and as a resident of old standing in the Transvaal, I do wish to submit to Your Lordship that the hardships that the present Ordinance would inflict upon us are unbearable. And I can assure Your Lordship that, immediately the Ordinance was introduced into the Legislative Council of the Transvaal, my fellow-countrymen felt, and felt very keenly, to think that such laws can be passed under a British Government. It is what I should never have believed years ago. Our lot is to-day infinitely worse than under the Boer *régime*; we were able to get protection from the British Government during that time. Are we now, under the same Government, to be persecuted? When aliens of all classes are, at the very moment that the Ordinance is introduced, pouring into the Transvaal, and when they enjoy all the rights and privileges granted to British subjects, my countrymen, who are always to the fore for the defence of the

Empire, are suffering these serious disabilities and the disabilities threatened by the Ordinance. To-day, in India, the frontier is guarded by my countrymen, who shoulder the rifle in defence of the Empire ; and it is very grievous that they should have to suffer such misery, and that there should be class-legislation against them of this type. I appeal for justice, and I appeal to Your Lordship, in the name of the British traditions, that you will be pleased to remove the disability that the Ordinance will place upon us, by vetoing it, or, at least, by granting a Commission. We are loyal British subjects, and, as such, we are entitled to the fullest protection. We have not asked for, and we do not now ask for, political rights ; we are content that the white man should be predominant in the Transvaal, but we do feel that we are entitled to all the other ordinary rights that a British subject should enjoy.

SIR HENRY COTTON.

SIR HENRY COTTON : I wish to say one word, my Lord, if I may. I am here not only as a retired Indian Official, like many distinguished men I see around me, but also as a member of the present Parliament and as Chairman of a meeting, which sat in the Grand Committee Room upstairs in the House of Commons, attended by more than 100 Members of the Liberal party. I take this opportunity of saying that I deeply regret that the invitations to attend that meeting were not extended to both sides of the House (Hear, hear). It was an unfortunate oversight, which we all regret. But that meeting, I say, was attended by 100 and more members of the House of Commons, and their feeling was very strong indeed upon this subject ; indeed, they went so far as to record a resolution that they sympathized with and supported the prayer of the petitioners. Since that meeting, My Lord, I have been brought in contact with many members of the House of Commons who were not present at the meeting, gentlemen on both sides of the House. Many gentlemen on the opposite benches have also intimated to me that there is a complete sympathy with the attitude taken up by Messrs, Gandhi and Ally on behalf of their fellow-subjects in the Transvaal.

I wish also, in associating myself, as I do completely, with the observations which fell from Sir Lepel Griffin, to remind your Lordship that it was Lord Lansdowne, for whom we all have the greatest regard and respect, who, although he is the leader of the Opposition in the House of Lords, is at all events, as we know very well, a most liberal-minded statesman, who drew prominent attention in England to the grievances which the British Indians in the Transvaal suffered from under President Kruger's administration. Nothing, he said, roused so much indignation in his mind, or so much anger as the ill-treatment which the British Indians received in South Africa. And he went further even in his speech—it was a speech delivered at Sheffield two or three weeks after the outbreak of war—for he said that he regarded with grave anxiety the state of feeling which must inevitably exist in India, when it was known that the British subjects of India in South Africa were so ill-treated and ground down. And he pointed out the imperative duty of the British Government to improve their status and position.

Now, My Lord, that was a pledge which was given by the head of the Opposition in the House of Lords, and I appeal to you, My Lord, as the representative of the Liberal Government, in dealing with this matter of South Africa, that your duty is at least as decisive as Lord Lansdowne claimed for himself a few years ago. It is true that the people of India do feel this matter very deeply. It is true also that the British Indians in South Africa have greater grievances to complain of now than they had under the Dutch Government, and the climax has been reached in the passing of this Ordinance of which Messrs. Gandhi and I here so grievously complain. Representing as I do a very influential and large section of the House of Commons, and I believe the almost unanimous official feeling in India on the subject, I do trust that Your Lordship will be able to give this petition your favourable consideration.

SIR M. BHOWNAGGREE.

SIR M. BHOWNAGGREE: My Lord, I think the case has been so ably and clearly put before Your Lordship that there is not the least occasion for me to go into any details, and if I feel called upon to address Your Lordship for a very few minutes, it is simply on account of the interest I took in this question all through my ten and a half years' career in Parliament. I want to bring to your Lordship's notice a few points which perhaps may not be within your knowledge.

In complaining of the grievances of British-Indian subjects in South Africa, I had opportunities of seeing your predecessors, Mr. Chamberlain and Mr. Lyttleton, very often on the subject. My activity had taken the form at last of a long printed letter, in which I detailed the whole narrative of the facts, and Mr. Lyttleton thereupon assured me that the case had been so fairly put, and the demands made so reasonable, that he hoped to get some relief. I, on the other hand, knew what the local forces of opposition to a liberal policy on the part of any Ministry of the Imperial Government would be, and whilst I thanked him for his sympathetic answer, I told him it might be necessary to appoint a Commission to inquire into the whole subject. Sir George Farrar, who represented the anti-British Indian interest in the Transvaal Legislature, also happened at the same time to suggest that the appointment of a Commission would ventilate the matter, and might bring some solution of that very difficult problem. Thereupon, I addressed Mr. Lyttleton again, accepting Sir George Farrar's offer, and matters were in that train, and I believe Mr. Lyttleton would have ultimately appointed a Commission, but the Government of which he was a member then, went out of office. Recognizing the very difficult position in which the whole question stands, I now urge that a Commission might be appointed, pending the report of which this Ordinance might at least be held in abeyance, so that you may have the benefit of judging the whole question by the report of that Commission.

I have only one word to add, my Lord. For five years Your Lordship has been the custodian and guardian of Indian interests, and the protector of their rights during a memorable and distinguished Viceroyalty. To-day as our leader, Sir Lepel Griffin, has well said, the eyes of all India are focussed on the proceedings which are taking place in this room, and I am only expressing the sentiments of the three hundred millions of people in India when I express the hope that Your Lordship will, on account of the sympathy which you have shown, and which I believe you are ready to show, and of which even on our entrance into this room you assured us, allow no other consideration but that of justice to weigh with you, and will grant the prayer which these gentlemen have come all this long distance here to ask at your hands.

MR. REES.

Mr. Rees: I am not going, my Lord, into the subject of the merits of the case. I think they were amply dealt with by Sir Lepel Griffin; nor am I going to speak of my interest in this subject, which I have often brought before Parliament myself, but when Sir Henry Cotton spoke of the meeting yesterday, I should like to say that it was not only a party meeting, but it was a meeting of a part of a party, and that I do deprecate with all my heart and soul, in a matter which is of such serious importance, any endeavour to make any subject connected with British India a party subject. I do not think that there can be a more serious matter than this very serious one upon which we have come before Your Lordship, viz.: the unfortunate manner in which our fellow-subjects have been treated in the Transvaal.

MR. HAROLD COX.

Mr. Harold Cox: My Lord, I am in a somewhat different position from most of the gentlemen here, because I am neither an ex-official of the Government of India, nor am I myself Indian by birth, but I did have the honour personally of serving in India for two years under a Native Prince, and I look back to that period of my life with the greatest pleasure. That is one special reason why I am here to-day. But at the back of my mind, the real reason why I am here to-day is because I am English, and because I think this matter is a disgrace to my country. Our country was pledged, when we went to war with the Transvaal, to do justice to the British Indians. That justice has not been done, and I contend that it is not possible for the present Government, of which Your Lordship is a part, to ride off on the plea that the Transvaal is a self-governing colony. It is not a self-governing colony. It is absolutely subject to your authority, and whatever is done by you to-day or at any other time, is done, not in the name of the Transvaal, but in the name of the English people, and in the name of the English people, I protest against any injustice being done to British subjects.

MR. NAOROJI.

MR. NAOROJI : I do not want to take up Your Lordship's time, and after the able manner in which the whole subject has been laid before you, I would only join in the appeal that has been made to you on behalf of my fellow-subjects under the British flag. If there is one principle more important than another, it is that of the freedom of British subjects under the British flag, and I do hope that the British Government, especially a Liberal Government, will stand upon this basis.

MR. AMEER ALI.

MR. AMEER ALI : Will Your Lordship allow me to make one observation only ? Perhaps my recent experience of India is the most recent of all. I venture to say this : that the feelings of India are very strong on this subject of the injury done to British Indians in the Transvaal, and it will be a serious mistake if the subject is put on one side. That is the only matter I want to present to Your Lordship.

LORD ELGIN'S REPLY.

THE EARL OF ELGIN: In the first place, I would like to say that I entirely accept the position which Mr. Cox put upon me. I am responsible, no doubt, for the advice which is given in this matter and nobody else, and I do not wish to shirk my responsibility. In the second place, I wish also to express my adherence to what was said by Mr. Rees, Sir Henry Cotton, and others, that I regard this as no party question at all. Sir Henry Cotton quoted from Lord Lansdowne, but I have before me a despatch from the Colonial Secretary of the last Government from which I should like to read one paragraph :

> " His Majesty's Government cannot believe that the British community in the Transvaal appreciate the true nature of the proposition which some of its members are pressing upon you. They, as Britons, are as jealous of the honour of the British name as ourselves, and even if a material sacrifice were necessary to vindicate that honour, I feel assured they would cheerfully make it. His Majesty's Government hold that it is derogatory to national honour to impose on resident British subjects disabilities against which we had remonstrated, and to which even the law of the late South African Republic rightly interpreted did not subject them, and they do not doubt that, when this is perceived, the public opinion of the colony will not any longer support the demand which has been put forward."

SIR HENRY COTTON: May I ask which Colonial Secretary that was?

THE EARL OF ELGIN: It was from Mr. Lyttleton, written in 1904.

Now I understand from the gentlemen who have come before me to-day that we are not here to discuss general sympathies, nor are we to consider anything further than the rights which the British-Indian communities possessed in the past. They do not ask at this present moment for an extension of those rights. That limits the matter, as I think you wish it to be limited, to the question of this Ordinance itself.

Sir Lepel Griffin: For the present, my Lord. We are going to fight the question hereafter.

The Earl of Elgin: Oh, yes, I am thinking of to-day, and the answer I have to give.

Sir Lepel Griffin: Yes.

The Earl of Elgin: I only make that observation in order that I may be precise in my answer. The question therefore is with reference to this Ordinance, and following up the remark I made just now about its being no party question, I hope you will accept it from me that it was no intention of the men at the head of the Transvaal Government—they distinctly stated so to me—that they had no intention whatever, in the legislation they brought forward, to do otherwise than to improve, rather than to make worse, the condition of the British-Indian community. I am not saying that the subject is not perfectly open to your criticisms, but I wish you to accept from me that that was the intention with which this legislation was brought forward. Now, Mr. Gandhi explains that, in some cases, for instance, in the case of the poll-tax, this concession which was supposed to be given under the Ordinance was illusory. I admit that I think there was something in his statement that most of those who would come under the restriction I have mentioned would probably have paid the £3. But at the same time, dealing with this as a matter of the status of the British Indians in the Transvaal, I can see that the Government might quite fairly have held that, in removing the imposition of the poll-tax once for all, they were *pro tanto* improving the status of the British Indians.

Then, with regard to the question of permits or registration, we have seen one of the permits given under the Boer

Administration. It is merely a receipt for the money. The Boer Administration, in that respect, as well as in a good many others, was not so accurate as the administration which necessarily, with our ideas, obtains under the British Government, and therefore I am only stating the view which has been put before me—the view of the Government of the Transvaal is this : that as it stood under the rules of the Boer Government, which they had inherited, there was great confusion and there were great administrative difficulties, and that, consequently, there was a considerable degree of friction and also there arose considerable delay in the determination of cases, of which I see traces in the petition itself. It was for that purpose, as I understand it, that the Government of the Transvaal proposed to constitute the form of registration ; but according to their representations to me, there was no intention whatever of making that form of registration in any way more oppressive than the form of permits properly administered. And, if I may just for a moment—I do not want to go into all details—follow this question of thumb-marks, I think that thumb-marks first came into notice prominently when Sir Henry Cotton and I were associated in the Government of India under our friend Mr. Henry, who occupies a prominent position in this City now. No doubt the imposition of thumb-marks was introduced in that case for the detection of criminals, but I do not know why the imposition of a thumb-mark in itself should be a very debasing operation. In fact, as they say, it has always seemed to me a most marvellous thing that they say they can trace every thumb-mark ; there might be an advantage over the hieroglyphics which some of us call our signatures. And there is this fact, I want just to mention, and to bring to the notice of Mr. Gandhi, that on the permit which he has handed to me issued under the present Ordinance, there is a thumb-mark already imposed under the present Ordinance in just the same way as it will be imposed under the new Ordinance.

MR. GANDHI : Only that that, as I said, is a purely

voluntary act done by us on the advice and the instigation of Lord Milner. He asked us to do that.

THE EARL OF ELGIN: Quite so; but still here is a certificate which is an official certificate, and it bears a thumb-mark.

LORD STANLEY OF ALDERLEY: It was affixed without prejudice.

THE EARL OF ELGIN: I do not see why it should not be affixed to the Registration certificate without prejudice.

SIR M. M. BHOWNAGGREE: Might I explain one thing here? Whatever Lord Milner asked British Indians to do was done on the understanding that the whole question of the treatment of the community was one of consideration between the Colonial Secretary for the time being, and Lord Milner and the local authorities; so that they might have submitted to Lord Milner's injunction in a respectful way, and, as Lord Stanley just now said, without prejudice. But this imposes a sort of distinction between one subject and another in the Transvaal.

THE EARL OF ELGIN: Do not suppose I am taking it further than this; I am only saying, here is a document which at present is in use with a thumb-mark and it cannot be called debasing.

MR. GANDHI: It is the " ten finger " mark.

THE EARL OF ELGIN: Is it more debasing with ten fingers?

SIR HENRY COTTON: It is only required in the case of criminals.

THE EARL OF ELGIN: I do not want to argue it, but I think there is just that much to be said. Then there is one matter about registration. That is, that if the system of registration was carried out, it would give a final and indefeasible title, to those who are registered, to their rights in the Transvaal. That is the position of the Transvaal Government on that matter. And as regards the carrying of a pass, and any oppressive use of the power of inspection, I am informed, and I have taken some trouble to ascertain it, that all that would be intended, so far as checking the Ordinance Certificate is concerned, is that it would probably be inspected once a year. As regards any other casual demand for it, it would be, as I am told, exactly in the same position as this permit is, which, if I am right, may be demanded from anybody in the Transvaal. That is the position. I do not want to elaborate too much on this subject; I only wish to make this explanation, that those were the sorts of reasons which the Government of the Transvaal put before me when they asked my assent to the introduction of the legislation on these grounds, and it is distinctly upon my apprehension that these modifications of the law would in the long run be for the benefit and not for the oppression of the British-Indian community, that I gave my assent to the introduction of that legislation. Now, gentlemen, we are in the position that this is challenged. I think I ought to say, without in any way challenging the authority with which Mr. Gandhi and Mr. Ali come here as the representatives of a large meeting, that I have got telegrams from the Transvaal advising me of the forwarding of a Petition from British Indians, which they say has been lately signed, in opposition to the views which have been placed before me to-day, and with regard to the general feeling I have to-day received two more telegrams—I say two more, because there are a good many others from different Municipalities in the country—urging the passing of the Ordinance, and so on. I cannot therefore entirely subscribe to what Sir Lepel Griffin said about the opposition, and the nature of the opposition, to this matter. I regret it more than anybody in this room. I suppose there could be found, if not in the records of this Office, at any rate in the records of the India Office, despatches, with my signature attached to them, protesting, in as strong language as has been used here, against the restrictions on British citizens, and I do not go back from one single word. But we have to recognize the fact that all over the world there are difficulties arising on the part of white communities, and we have to reckon with them.

I do not say that they ought always to succeed; they certainly ought not to succeed in points of detail which would in any way involve oppression. But the fact of there being that sentiment has to be borne in mind when we have to deal with matters of this description. I do not think I have much more to reply to. A reference has been made to the proposition, towards the end of the Petition, that at any rate there might be a postponement for the examination of the subject by a Commission. That, no doubt, is an alternative which might be adopted; but I am not in a position to-day to say whether that is so or not. Indeed, I think you will easily acknowledge that I did you the best compliment when I did not endeavour to make up my mind until I had seen you and heard what you have to say. That is my position: I have now heard what Mr. Gandhi had to say. I hope he has put before me as fully as he desired what he had come so far to say. I have heard the other gentlemen who have accompanied him. I will give the best consideration to their representations, and I shall think it my duty to make up my mind with the full responsibility which I have to assume.

Mr. Gandhi: May I make one statement, my Lord, for one minute? I have listened with the very greatest attention, and with very great obligation, to Your Lordship's statement, but I must submit that the information placed before Your Lordship on some points is not accurate, and I am in a position to refute that information by documentary evidence with regard to permits, as Your Lordship used the term in connexion with the Ordinance of 1885, but this is not the occasion when I could do it. But if your Lordship will ask us to wait upon you, we will do it. But that just shows that nothing short of a Commission would place our position accurately before Your Lordship.

Sir Lepel Griffin: My Lord, I beg, on behalf of the Deputation, to express our best thanks for the exceedingly kind and courteous way in which you have received us, and the patience with which you have listened to what we had to say. We were assured before of your full sympathy in this matter, and knew it perfectly well.

The Deputation then withdrew.

INDEX